I'm Not Suffering from INSANITY...
I'm Enjoying Every Minute of It!

I'm Not Suffering from INSANITY...

I'm Enjoying Every Minute of It!

KAREN SCALF LINAMEN

Fleming H. Revell

A Division of Baker Book House Co
Grand Rapids, Michigan 49516

Published by Fleming H. Revell
a division of Baker Book House Company
P.O. Box 6287, Grand Rapids, MI 49516-6287

Second printing, March 2003

Printed in the United States of America

Library of Congress Cataloging-in-Publication Data

Linamen, Karen Scalf, 1960–
    I'm not suffering from insanity—I'm enjoying every minute of it! /
Karen Scalf Linamen.
        p.   cm.
    ISBN 0-8007-5781-5 (pbk.)
    1. Christian women—Conduct of life. I. Title.
BV4527 .L548 2002
248.8'42—dc21   2002006203

Portions of chapter 8 originally appeared in *Today's Christian Woman*, March/April 2001.

Interior illustrations by Steve Björkman

For current information about all releases from Baker Book House, visit our web site:
http://www.bakerbooks.com

For the women who read my books,
particularly those of you who send me stories
from your lives
and pieces of your hearts via e-mail and snail mail.
I consider you friends, each and every one.

Contents

∙∙

Acknowledgments

My heartfelt thanks to the talented folks at Revell, with special thanks to editor Lonnie Hull DuPont. My agent, Linda Holland, remains a cheerleader, shrewd business partner, and friend. My gratitude to John Smeltzer, to put it simply, eclipses words. My family and friends keep me sane, and even when that task gets the best of them they manage to love me anyway, which is about as good as it can possibly get. Everyone should be so blessed.

Introduction

···

One day I was talking to my sister Renee when I said, "I feel like I'm going to have a nervous breakdown."

Renee said, "Please don't do that! Then you'd be sad all the time. Go insane instead. You'll never know the difference!"

Do you ever feel like that? Like life is just one big padded room? I'm thinking that you must because here we are again, you and I, rendezvousing over yet another book dedicated to those seasons in our lives when we feel like socks being tossed without mercy in the spin cycle of life.

The bad news is that life throws us for a loop now and then.

The good news is that there's something we can do when it happens.

Like *Just Hand Over the Chocolate and No One Will Get Hurt,* this book is filled with fourteen things you and I can do that will make a positive difference in our lives emotionally, physically, or spiritually.

And like *Sometimes I Wake Up Grumpy . . . and Sometimes I Let Him Sleep,* the purpose of this book is to help you—and me too—experience greater joy, purpose, passion, and healing in our lives.

Between all three books, there are more than four dozen practical ways to lift our spirits when we find ourselves in an emotional crisis for any reason including stress, depression, PMS, or the fact that we just went out and bought our very first bottle of Rogaine For Women.

Sometimes I think, *How many ways to feel better can there possibly be? Surely I'll run out of material soon!* But then I hit a new bump in the road of life, or meet up with an unexpected angel, or experience a miracle, or learn how to laugh at something that only a short time ago would have made me bawl, and I realize there's more to say on this subject after all.

So here we are. And I, for one, am thrilled for your company.

Together, you and I are going to talk about speeding tickets, tube tops, and the therapeutic benefits of the perfect shade of lipstick.

We're going to examine several dozen ways to make a new friend, as well as how to go back in time and reclaim a healthy friendship that got lost along the way.

We're also going to talk about . . .

© the kind of muscle we need to budge those grudges right out of our lives . . .

© how the right lingerie can lift our moods . . .

© and the appropriate time to spritz hair spray on a spider.

And if you've ever wished you could redecorate a room for less than a hundred bucks, or felt so wounded by life that you're not even sure there's a God, or wondered what kind of woman could get *both* her lips caught in a car door, or had a hard time forgiving yourself for something you really, really regret . . . then that's all the more reason why this is the perfect book for you.

I wish I could make your life perfect and easy and sane (almost as much as I wish you could do the same for me!). But since I can't, at least we can laugh together, cry together, and swap stories from the padded room.

Are you ready to experience greater joy, gratitude, beauty, satisfaction, and hope in your life? Yeah, me too. Let's do it together, shall we? Let's fling wide our hearts and arms and begin this very moment to embrace some of the best that life has to offer.

Of course, it's possible that you're thinking, *She doesn't know what she's asking!* Or even, *How can I possibly embrace those things?*

But I believe that together we can make it happen. Together we can do it. So let's not let anything stop us, shall we?

Not even these straitjackets.

1

Make a Friend...Again

There's lots of stuff I *don't* miss in my life.

Remember eight tracks?

How about sticky lip gloss?

Here's a good one—what about those elastic belts that held our "feminine hygiene" products in place? Miss those? Neither do I.

Braces.

Rotary dial phones.

How 'bout eighties-style big hair?

I have a few regrets in life, but losing my lacquered big hair and blue eye shadow aren't among the bunch.

Some things you're just better off without.

Maybe it's the lateness of the hour (I'm writing at midnight, my kids asleep, dishwasher loaded, dog fed, lunches made). Or maybe the culprit is what happened last week when I went home for Christmas—I'll tell you about it in a few minutes. But whatever the reason, I'm sitting here thinking about things lost, some of which, like the "gems" in the list above, have left my life richer with their absence.

Other things may have left my life all right, but the word *richer* doesn't exactly apply. In fact, their absence leaves me downright sad.

Bladder control comes to mind. I happen to have a cold at the moment. It has settled in my chest, which means that every few minutes I erupt into energetic coughing. You might be wondering what this has to do with bladder control. Actually, you're only wondering if you happen to be in your teens or twenties. If you're a forty-something woman like me with a couple of childbirths under your belt, you know exactly what I'm talking about.

My eyebrows. That's another one. I miss my eyebrows. The older I get, the thinner they get. Except I did something recently that's actually helping me not miss my brows so much. I had permanent makeup applied to my brows. Tattooed, really. Kind of like penciling in the perfect brows, except it's forever. These babies will outlast a Maytag washer. You can dig me up after I'm gone and I'll look sort of like the stuff you see when you empty the bag on your vacuum, but you'll take one look at me and say, "Well, she *does* still have great brows."

What else do I miss? To be honest, there are a handful of friendships that have come and gone in my life and have left me sort of empty in their wake.

Have you ever had something like that happen in your life? You're super close to someone and you think you'll never know a day when you don't feel the same way, and then something happens and you bicker, or you drift, or someone moves, or something changes, and suddenly you've lost that connection and you think about it sometimes and regret the loss and wish you could get it back.

Earlier I referred to something that happened when I went home for Christmas, and it has to do with this very subject, with friendship lost. But before we get too sad, let me just say that sometimes you get a second chance. Sometimes it's possible to go back and pick up a thread that leads you to a strand that can take you to a remnant of strings still tied to the heart of someone you lost.

I'll tell you all about it in a moment. But first I need to take a break. I need to get something from the cabinet above the bathroom sink. That's where I keep the cold medicine. I've got to take something for this cough. In fact, as long as I'm up I think I'll hunt around for anything else that might make me more comfortable until I get over this annoying, hacking cough.

Now where in the world did I put those elastic belts . . .

Let Your Fingers Do the Walking

Okay, I'm back. Now, on to the story about what happened at Christmastime.

It all started when my sister Michelle blurted, "Let's call Brenda. Right now. Don't even think about it! Let's just do it."

We were in Michelle's home office. She was sitting by her computer. I was across the desk from her, painting my nails. I looked up. "Really? Now? After seven years?"

We had once been really close, the three of us. The silly nicknames and private jokes we shared could have filled volumes. We grew up together, really, and at one time the good memories had run as freely as milk and honey.

Then seven years ago something happened. Not a fight, really, just a concentrated time of stress and transition, and before we could smooth everything out, Brenda's divorce swept her down her own private path of emotional crisis, and my struggles with clinical depression swept me in an entirely different direction. As for Michelle, she had her hands full as she married, separated for a season, rebuilt a great marriage, and had a baby. As sisters, Michelle and I stayed close, of course, but we lost Brenda in the process. The threads of communication had snapped, and we had spun completely out of each other's orbits.

Michelle didn't blink an eye, "Yeah. Right now. After seven years. I'll dial."

I held the cordless extension gingerly with wet fingernails and watched Michelle dial the other phone.

Ring.

Ring.

Ring.

Michelle said, "Hi, Brenda, this is a voice from your past."

"Hello?"

Michelle said, "Hi, Brenda, this is a voice from your past."

I said, "Two voices."

Brenda said, "I have no idea who you are. Who is this?"

Michelle said, "You have to guess. We wanted to say hi. We miss you."

Brenda said, "You DO sound sorta familiar . . ."

I said, "I see we're going to have to sing."

Michelle said, "Sing?"

I said, "Yes, sing. You know the song. Ready? One, two, three . . ."

So we sang "Burn, Cookie, Burn." You can stop trying to recall the tune from some national countdown. The only time and place it has ever been performed is around midnight in the orange and gold kitchen in my parents' house on Farm Street back in the mid-'70s. You see, Brenda, Michelle, and I were baking cookies when we began pretending the cookies were talking to us from the oven and—

No. We weren't on drugs. We were teenagers and punchy with life and with the lateness of the hour, and it really did seem pretty hysterical at the time, and I'm not even going to TRY to explain it for one more second. You just have to believe me. It was funny at the time.

And somehow, it was funny again last week, when Brenda's voice suddenly broke into laughter and we heard her squeal, "You GUYS, what ARE you doing?" and the tentative tendrils of reconnection touched and caught and held, and suddenly we were kids again and friends.

It was a very good moment.

And I have Michelle to thank for it.

It takes courage to reach out across a rift. Michelle was brave. And wise. More so than I. I just got to tag along and reap the benefits.

We met the next day for lunch. Brenda saw photos of Michelle's baby and met my five-year-old for the first time. Her son, Blake, had been six months old when I'd seen him last—now there are hockey trophies on his bedroom walls.

I think we'll hang on better this time. I also think we were lucky. I think second chances are too special to squander.

No Regrets

There's an old adage: "Fish and houseguests begin to stink after three days."

You know what else stinks the longer it hangs around?

Regret.

In fact, regret does more than stink. Regret can make you crazy.

Now, I'm not suggesting that you and I should live perfect lives. I'm not saying that we should be able to manage our days on earth so perfectly that we never do or say anything that we wish we could reverse.

The fact is, life is messy and chaotic and imperfect, and sometimes things happen that we'd give our eyeteeth to correct. Sometimes what we regret is something we said or did or didn't do. We'd give anything if we had seen the doctor sooner, finished our degree, said "no" to temptation or "I love you" when we had the chance, lightened up, straightened up, or buckled up, married a first love, or heeded a warning sign along the way.

Other times, what we regret is not anything we did but something someone else did to us. Either way, regrets are unavoidable. If we have a pulse, you and I are going to have some regrets in life. And if we let those regrets eat us alive, we're going to need a straitjacket for sure.

Dealing with Unfortunate Good-Byes

We've all met women who can't seem to get past a regret in life. They're consumed by bitterness, defined by a past mistake. They've let regret drive them nuts, and they can't seem to forget and move on.

This chapter isn't about *every* category of regret in our lives (that would require a book, not a chapter!). But I figured I could talk about at least one kind of regret and offer some ideas on how to keep it from gnawing away at your innards for years.

I'm talking, of course, about the kind of regret that occurs when a good relationship goes awry.

For example, I lost Brenda when stress tested our relationship and (at least for me) personal struggles kept me too busy to reconnect.

I seem to have lost the Rottmeyers and the Spurlocks when these two families moved away last summer. Nancy and Larry headed to Indiana, and Cherie and her family moved to Colorado, and though I've missed them daily, I haven't exactly been burning up the phone lines keeping in touch. Yes, the distance is a factor. But I also think their leaving left a painful void in my life, and when I'm hurting I tend to withdraw and regroup and heal. Now, several months later, I'm feeling less vulnerable and more aware of my need to reach out again. Keeping in touch over the miles takes some effort, but I think I'm gearing up for the challenge.

I lost Chris, another friend, over some stupid stuff. I offended this friend last year, and things have never been the same. I called once and sent a couple e-mails containing apologies, but they have yet to be answered. It makes me sad. It's a loss I truly regret.

Some relationships end, and it's just as well. Perhaps there was something in the relationship that was unhealthy or toxic or wounding. Other relationships were good for years before something got twisted and they crashed and burned. I'm not suggesting that every ended relationship be renewed. But I guess I'm saying that—for the healthy ones—if time or events or conflict or distance have created a rift that you regret, what's wrong with going back and making amends, re-creating the connection, renewing a bond?

Here are some suggestions on how to do just that.

Let Your Fingers Do the Walking

Sometimes all it takes is a phone call. I know, for example, that despite the miles between us, Nancy and Cherie are a mere phone call away. I'll be the first to admit that when I've been remiss at keeping in touch, I'm tempted to put off the phone call, thinking, *But it's been months. Will they be upset with me? Will it be awkward? Will they ask why I've been silent for so long?* And yet, in my heart of hearts, I know the answer. These are rock-solid friendships. The connection we shared remains untarnished. So what if their leaving left me a little numb and I needed some time to heal? Great. Fine. Now it's time to get busy and reconnect and reinvest and reclaim. What about you? Do you have a good relationship you've let slide? Then pick up the phone. Today. And I promise I'm going to do the same. Because good friends are hard to come by and too priceless to be allowed to drift casually beyond our reach.

> Some relationships end, and it's just as well. Other relationships were good for years before something got twisted and they crashed and burned.

Say You're Sorry

If you've made a mistake and hurt someone, ask for forgiveness. If you're not sure, say so by admitting something like,

"If I offended you in some way, I'm really sorry. Tell me what I've done so we can talk about it, because your friendship has always been important to me and I'd hate to lose it now."

You'll feel better when you apologize, regardless of whether your apology jump-starts the friendship again or not. I wish that my apology had jump-started my friendship with Chris. So far, it hasn't. I'm still glad I apologized. It was something I needed to do, regardless of the outcome.

Kill a Grudge

Sometimes what's standing between you and reclaiming a former good friend is the fact that, frankly, you're still ticked. Was the offense done in malice? Was it part of an unhealthy pattern that characterized your relationship? Was it brutal enough to tarnish your feelings for your friend forever?

If not, I have three little words for you: "Get over it."

I explain this to my daughters all the time. I tell them that good girlfriends are hard to come by, and even the best relationships require a generous application of grace now and then.

> Sometimes what's standing between you and reclaiming a former good friend is the fact that, frankly, you're still ticked.

Guard Your Expectations

When you attempt to rekindle a friendship, consider your mission accomplished if you get one good conversation out of it all. If you contact an old friend expecting that your relationship will immediately bloom into all that it was before time/conflict/distance created a wedge between you, you may be disappointed. People change, circumstances change, schedules change. It's quite possible that your friendship, even if it gets renewed, will be different than it was before.

Maybe your friend has a husband now, or you have a new baby. Perhaps she lives twelve hundred miles away instead of right next door. It's possible that one of the two of you is busier than you were before and quality time will have to suffice when quality and quantity used to be the rule of thumb. Perhaps you'll become best friends again, or maybe you'll merely swap Christmas letters once a year. It's also possible that your conversation won't open the door for bosom-buddyhood but will bring about good stuff just the same, stuff like forgiveness, healing, resolution, or just even an hour's worth of warm fuzzies.

Relationships evolve, and that's okay. The goal is not to relive the past but to write a new chapter in a relationship with someone who shares part of your history. Let that new chapter unfold as it may.

Friendship 911

Do you regret losing a once-healthy friendship to distance, time, or an unfortunate misunderstanding? Sometimes it's possible to go back and pick up a thread of a remnant of strings still tied to the heart of someone you lost. If you want to reclaim a former friendship, here are some suggestions:

◎ Evaluate whether the relationship was basically healthy. If it was dysfunctional or destructive in some way, think carefully—and perhaps even seek wise counsel—before trying to resurrect the connection.
◎ Be willing to apologize for anything you did that caused the friendship to falter.
◎ Be willing to forgive if you're the one nurturing the grudge.
◎ Guard your expectations. People and circumstances change. Don't expect your relationship to pick up exactly where you left it.
◎ Don't guard your affection. Be honest! If you've missed your friend . . . if you regret the time spent apart . . . if you'd give anything to share a box of chocolates and some girltalk like you used to . . . say it!

Don't Guard Your Affection

When you contact your old friend, it's okay to guard your expectations, but don't guard your affection in the process. Be honest. Talk freely. Nix the guessing games. Set the tone early by admitting, "I miss you!" Your transparency will go a long way toward rekindling the bond that once was strong.

There are lots of reasons to patch up, reclaim, or renew good relationships gone stale. For one thing, the older I get the more I recognize and appreciate past relationships that, at their very core, were solid and healthy. Sometimes reconnecting with this kind of friend or family member just feels right. Other times unfinished business calls our names.

Whatever the reason, sometimes rekindling a friendship is very good. Besides, after so much time apart, there's always lots of news to share, everything from the earth-shattering to the interesting to, well . . . the bizarre.

I can't wait to tell Brenda about my eyebrows.

2

....

Practice Your Passions

L et me tell you what does NOT evoke my passion.

Getting up in the morning, for starters. I am not one of those people who leaps out of bed bright-eyed and bushy-tailed. It's more like bushy-eyed and dim-witted.

I hate mornings and I let it show.

My sister's husband had the chance to witness this for himself one morning while I was staying at their house. Moments after forcing myself out of bed, I passed him in the hallway on the way to the bathroom. I was stumbling along with one eye open and one still closed, wearing flannel pajamas and a scowl.

At breakfast I told my sister, "Be nice to Russ today. He had a rough morning. He saw me right after I got up."

Michelle turned to her husband. "Was it bad?"

Russ thought a moment before answering as diplomatically as he could, "Your sister in the morning could cure hiccups."

So you can see that mornings aren't exactly my passion.

Neither is housework. My house is a busy place that brims with two kids, their friends, my husband, my friends, my home office, and one white German shepherd named Walter. In other words, this old place gets a lot of wear and tear, and I don't exactly follow everyone around with a dustpan and broom.

For example, in my kitchen alone, I have not one but three junk drawers. There is also a junk basket on the counter containing, among other things, a Christmas ornament made of felt and pretzels, a Rugrats toothbrush, some Chuck E Cheese's arcade tickets, five pairs of sunglasses, a dozen Pixie Sticks, sidewalk chalk, a phone bill, three tic-tac containers (all empty), an envelope of hollyhock seeds, several spools of green thread, a three-inch plastic dog, and a can of mystery food with the label torn off.

My husband's in the doghouse. Not that he seems to mind. Maybe it's because our dog is a better housekeeper than I am.

I try to keep this place picked up and clean, I really do. It's just that I rarely succeed. Still, just because I can admit it myself doesn't mean I enjoy hearing about it from anyone else.

Last week we bought a new TV. As my husband, Larry, started to slide the old one out of the entertainment center, he looked behind the set and said, "Wow. What's it called when dust gets so thick it starts to pile up on itself?"

I said, "Dust bunnies."

He said, "I think these must be dust goats."

So now he's in the doghouse. Not that he seems to mind. Maybe it's because our dog is a better housekeeper than I am. That's because every time eighty-two-pound Walter wags his tail he knocks the vicinity clear of anything in his way, dust goats, small appliances, and compact vehicles included.

Now THAT'S what I call passion.

Passion Brings Good Things to Life

Life has its share of drudgery. It brims with mundane work we've got to do to keep things running. Folding laundry, paying bills, making school lunches, balancing checkbooks, washing dishes, and corralling dust bunnies are a few examples from my life that come to mind.

I don't feel energized when I'm doing these chores. In fact, I have to work pretty hard to stay focused on the responsibilities that fail to evoke my passion. I can do it, of course. I'm just saying it requires a lot of commitment and effort.

Not like when there's passion. Nosiree. Passion creates another story altogether.

There's something amazing about passion. It has a life of its own. Passion animates. It energizes. It's better than General Electric because not only does it bring good things to life, there's no utility bill to pay at the end of the month.

Passion is beautiful to watch.

I saw some last week. I was talking to my friend Jeanette. She was telling me how she was trying to figure out how to stay a step ahead of depression and infuse more joy into her life at the same time. Assuming that exercise would help, she was thinking of joining a gym. Wondering if new scenery would help, she was considering attending a ladies' retreat. Hoping that getting out of the house would help, she had planned a few lunches with friends.

A few moments later, the conversation drifted. One of us mentioned e-mail, and Jeanette started talking about how she loves to send cards and messages to her friends, and suddenly her face was glowing.

I mean it. Glowing.

I reached for my sunglasses and encouraged her to keep talking.

She did. She talked nonstop for fifteen minutes about how much she loves sending long letters to people telling them how special they are. She said some of her favorite words are *precious, cherished,* and *valued.* She said what she writes are love letters, really, and she writes them to her husband, kids, friends, pastor, colleagues, and neighbors. She's even wondered what would happen if she started writing them to mere acquaintances, near strangers. Would they feel bewildered or encouraged? She's fascinated by the power of the written word to lift and to edify, and crafting masterpieces of edifying prose is something she could do for hours without thinking twice.

I said, "So, when you're done writing a letter like this, do you feel energized or drained?"

I had to squint at the light emanating from her face.

She said, "I feel GREAT."

> Jeanette didn't swallow a lightbulb. She had merely pinpointed one of her passions, and the resulting energy and animation were startling.

I said, "Jeanette, the gym is nice. The ladies' retreat is nice. Lunch with friends is nice. But if you want to feel better, have more energy, and get more enjoyment out of your life, set aside some time every single day, turn on your computer, and get busy and WRITE SOME LETTERS!"

She wasn't convinced. She said, "Really? You think that would help?"

My face was sunburned from just sitting in the same room with her. I said, "Trust me on this one."

Pinpoint Your Passions

Jeanette didn't swallow a lightbulb. She had merely pinpointed one of her passions, and the resulting energy and animation were startling.

How I'd love to bottle up some of that energy and animation and put it on the market. Imagine! One swig and it would be "Good-bye, depression," "Good-bye, boredom," "Good-bye, fatigue," "Good-bye, drudgery."

Okay, maybe not "good-bye" for good, but at least "ta ta for now."

Look. If you and I are searching for ways to enrich our lives and experience greater joy in our days, pinpointing and pursuing our passions might not be a bad place to start.

Indeed, the same passion that filled Jeanette with such energy and animation can flow from you and me as well. We just have to identify what we love.

I pinpointed one of my passions not long ago. I was in counseling and complaining to my friend and Christian counselor, John, that some days it felt like my life was little more than a conglomeration of responsibilities. I said, "Some days I'm not even sure who I am. You know, the real me, outside of my titles and roles."

He said, "That's easy. Tell me what you love."

It took me a few minutes to figure out what he meant. I thought a while, then said, "I think I love words. Words and ideas. I love talking about concepts and solutions and the process of figuring things out. Analyzing. Brainstorming. Delving into matters of life and love and uncovering the workings of the heart and soul. Long conversations about things, intangible things, things that really matter. Just figuring it all out. Making sense of it all."

My words had started out slow but soon were tumbling out in a rush, and before long I felt myself begin to glow. I felt my own transformation, felt an energy spreading inside, and I knew that, yes, this was something I really loved.

Since then I've thought a lot about passion. I've looked for signs of it in my own life and in the lives of folks around me too. I think that's why I enjoyed watching the transformation in Jeanette.

And when it comes to my other friends, well, here's what I've noticed. I've noticed, for example, that while my friend Condall is well versed on many topics, his voice starts to glow when he talks about Baylen, his son.

If you want to get my friend Cherie going, just ask her about the teenagers she loves to teach and disciple through her church and in her home.

When Darrell gets talking about going to battle to win a better life for folks with disabilities, you'd think his pants were on fire.

My brother-in-law Russ is just a normal guy until you get him on the subject of telling people about Jesus. Then transformation starts to happen, and the next thing you know, there's an excitement in his eyes that looks an awful lot like lightning.

Don't ask Kathy about her dogs Aspen and Sugar (or get her on any animal-related topic) unless you're free for a while.

My daughter Kaitlyn is amazing. Mention the Texas Rangers and she'll start spouting batting averages and stats and stories and opinions about trades and calls like she was born in a dugout. She videotapes every game. She clips and saves articles from the sports page. I keep waiting for her to start chewing tobacco and adjusting her crotch, but so far so good.

I have a friend named Brad. He's pretty laid back. Mr. Joe Cool. My family has known him for nearly thirty years. But apparently there's a side of Brad we had never seen before. At Christmastime, we were all hanging out at my parents' house when my dad said, "Hey, Brad, I need a favor. I've got some business records I want to put on Excel, but I can't figure out the software. You're good with numbers; help me out here."

Two hours later my dad emerged from his home office. There was a dazed but happy gleam in his eye. He said, "Brad's still at it. He's amazing. He loves this stuff. Can you picture how a concert pianist is with his music? That's Brad, on the computer with these numbers. He's completely immersed. He's inside of it, and it's inside of him, and it's beautiful to see."

So here's a question. What do you love? What ignites your fire? What animates your spirit and sends your words tumbling and invigorates your imagination? Maybe there's one major thing. Most likely there are several things that evoke your passion to varying degrees.

Pinpoint your passions. Then let's put them to work in your life. I've identified three ways to put your passions to work for you. Let's take a look.

1. Let Passion Maximize Your Problem-Solving

For years I've been making lists of ways to improve my life, and for years my lists have looked like this:

_ Go on a diet and lose 20 pounds
   (I hate to diet.)

_ Make beds
_ Mop kitchen floor
_ Do two loads of laundry
_ Windex French doors
_ Easy-Off my oven
   (Housework puts me to sleep.)

_ 7:45–8:15 Answer e-mails
_ 8:15–9:30 Return business calls
_ 9:30–11:30 Finish rewriting chapter 7
_ 12:30–2:30 Begin research for next set of columns
   (I am structure-impaired and don't even wear a watch.)

Is it any wonder I never manage to get my life together?

The bottom line is that for years I've been creating to-do lists of things I don't enjoy and at which I am not particularly gifted—and then I wonder why I never have any success!

Some people are disciplined. Some people can fill their days with activities they hate to do, then grit their teeth and plow through by sheer willpower.

I'm not one of them. It's possible that you're not either.

So lately I've been thinking.

What if you and I stopped making lists of what we think we SHOULD be doing . . . and made lists of what we LOVED to do instead? What if we stopped listing our priorities and started living our passions? What would our lives be like then?

Now don't get me wrong. I'm not saying we should neglect our responsibilities. I'm not advocating that we abandon our obligations. And I'm certainly not suggesting that we live for ourselves and pursue only what feels good in light of our whims and desires.

What if we stopped listing our priorities and started living our passions?

Not at all. Instead, I'm suggesting that we pinpoint our passions and use them to accomplish our goals, dreams, and responsibilities in a way that leaves us energized and satisfied at the same time.

What do I love? In addition to words and ideas, I love people—I crave interaction with folks I care about. I also love entertaining—nothing motivates me like throwing a party! And when I stick with it for a while and hit my stride, I can also get pretty passionate about working out. Strength-training, to be exact. Hefting all those weights and watching my strength increase and my body get toned get me pretty fired up.

What if, with this in mind, I made a NEW kind of list for my life, one that embraced my passions whenever possible? What might that look like? Let's see . . .

⊚ **Throw away my scale and work out instead, inviting friends along when possible.** What if I took my focus off the numbers on my scale and instead paid attention to the changes in my body that occur when I put in hours at the weight bench and treadmill? And knowing how I enjoy my friends, what if I worked out with a girlfriend whenever possible? With this in mind, I recently talked my friend Jenni into taking belly dancing lessons with me, and I'm trying to talk Michelle, Cherie, Nancy, Darla, and Beth into training with me for the Avon 3-Day Walk for Breast Cancer. Now *that's* motivating.

◎ **Entertain once a week.** Several months ago I had an interesting experience: I'd intended all week to clean my house but of course never got around to it. Then on Saturday, Condall and Kathy Clegg called and wanted to get together. I invited them over for Kentucky Fried Chicken and frozen cheesecake. In the single hour before they arrived, I washed dishes, vacuumed carpets, stashed toys, and Windexed the dog slobber off the French doors. I set the table, put on a pot of green beans, and popped a load of laundry in the washing machine—and I enjoyed every minute of it! Bottom line, I love to entertain, and the thought of having friends in my home lights a fire under me like nothing else. How can I make this passion work for me? What if I nixed extensive lists of daily chores and—every three or four days—invited a girlfriend, couple, or family into my home? Passion really does make a difference.

◎ **Brainstorm whenever possible.** All it takes is an hour or two of brainstorming words and ideas with folks like Linda Holland or Keith Wall, and I'm stoked for a couple days. I really do energize off interaction with family, friends, and folks in my industry. Unfortunately, my work tends to isolate me, unless of course you consider a German shepherd and a cup of coffee stimulating human companionship, which I don't. To make this passion work for me, perhaps I can nix the minutia-based schedule and begin my days instead by brainstorming with a pal. Keith and I have talked about meeting weekly to discuss the novel we want to write together, and Linda always brims with great ideas. A little de-isolation gets me energized, and if I work it right, I think I can channel some of that energy into my work.

Do you want help when it comes to improving your life? Meeting your goals? Managing your day? Then put your passions to work for you. Pinpoint three or four activities that you love, then find ways to incorporate them into your life. Use your passions—just like I did—to solve problems, meet goals, and address responsibilities in your life.

2. Let Passion Revolutionize Your Career

I've always been passionate about writing. I was writing poetry when I was five. I started a neighborhood magazine when I was twelve. I served on yearbook and newspaper staffs throughout my days at Warren High School and Biola University. I'm lucky. I found a way to turn my passion into a living.

You may not have been so lucky. But don't despair. It's not necessarily too late to turn your passion into your career.

Let me tell you about Jason. For years, Jason worked for the city where I live. He was employed by the Department of Parks and Recreation. His job was to keep all the Little League ball fields looking great. Nice job except for one thing.

He hated it.

One day he thought, *If I don't take a chance and make a change, I'm going to be doing this when I'm sixty.*

Several weeks later a casual comment from a friend helped him pinpoint a passion and pointed him to his new career. Jason explains: "I'd always had a reputation for giving great back rubs. One day I was giving back rubs to my wife and her best friend when the friend said, 'You should be doing this professionally,' and I decided, 'Well, why not?'"

Jason checked into some schools and nine months later began a new career as a licensed massage therapist. Today he says, "I never thought going to work every morning could be so much fun! I love what I do and am thrilled I made the change."

3. Let Passion Energize Your Pastimes

It's one thing to use your passions to manage your day or make a living. But you don't need an excuse to enjoy more passionate living. Your entire life can feel energized when you pursue your passions as hobbies or avocations.

You're probably thinking, *But I don't have the time or energy to raise koi. Or to Jazzercise. Or to take gourmet cooking lessons.* My advice? Do them anyway. I say this because, if you feel passionate about these things, doing them may quite possibly leave you more energized than before you began. Indeed, passion creates energy. Passionate living can add zest to your life like nothing else. It requires some effort, but it's an investment that can reap dividends far beyond your wildest dreams.

When we wake up our passions, we just might wake up our lives.

So pick a hobby, any hobby. Just make sure it's something you're crazy about, and watch your lackluster days begin to shine.

If Jeanette, Jason, and others can do it, so can you and I. By filling our lives with relationships and activities that we love, we'll not only feel better, we'll have more energy and joy as well.

If we want our days to soar instead of plod, the solution is simple: When we wake up our passions, we just might wake up our lives.

And if all that waking up occurs midmorning or later, well, all the better.

I may be passionate about a lot of things, but curing hiccups isn't necessarily one of them.

3

···

Slay One Dragon

I'm not particularly good at killing things.

Except, of course, houseplants. Houseplants and maybe time. I'm fairly skilled at killing time. But other than plants and time, I don't kill a whole lot.

Not even bugs are afraid of me. And why should they be? I don't kill bugs. I make my husband kill them.

When it comes to bugs, my husband is actually a little scary. When I was a new bride of merely weeks, I asked him to kill a spider on the stucco wall in our bedroom. Larry agreed, then approached the spider with an empty wastebasket in one hand and a can of hair spray in the other.

I have to admit, I was intrigued.

He explained, "See how textured the wall is? If I squash him on the wall, we'll never get him off. Well, not all of him anyway. I've got to knock him into this wastebasket before I can kill him."

It dawned on me that he might be enjoying this a little too much.

Positioning the wastebasket under the spider, he gave the arachnid a quick spray with the VO5. Startled (I'm speculating, of course), the spider dropped into the empty basket and began running in circles.

A moment later, Larry was seated on the edge of the bed, the wastebasket on the floor between his feet, a bottle of clear nail polish in his hands.

I said, "What in the world are you doing with my nail polish?"

He said, "I'm going to paint him and see how long it takes for him to harden up."

He WAS enjoying this a little too much. I wondered what other maniacal schemes lurked in the nefarious corners of the mind of the man I had married.

I slept with the lights on after that.

But back to killing.

If I can't even kill a spider, how in the world am I supposed to slay a dragon?

It's possible that I'm thinking about dragons because last night I stayed up past midnight reading *Beowulf: A New Verse Translation* by Seamus Heaney. I don't mean to sound all literate and highbrow, but it's a cool story and a very engaging translation. I even read portions to Kacie.

But my point is that I was up late reading about this guy named Beowulf and how he slew three different dragons before suffering a mortal blow in the third and final battle. Which might be why I'm thinking of dragons this morning.

But I don't think Beowulf is entirely to blame. I say this because I often feel as though there are dragons lurking in the darker corners of my life. Okay, maybe not dragons per se, but large fire-breathing carnivores, and they're waiting to pounce when I'm least suspecting the attack.

Alright, so they're not really carnivores. But they loom over me just the same, whispering dark threats and murmuring of worst-case scenarios. At first glance, they don't look all that scary. In fact, on the surface, they look pretty innocuous. They look like, well, everyday objects like an unpaid bill or an unmet deadline that is fast approaching (or maybe has already passed!). Some of my dragons look, on the surface, uncannily like a phone call I've been putting off for months or that doctor's appointment I keep promising to make.

Ever encounter a dragon in your life? Something unpleasant lurking over your shoulder? Something you've been neglecting, delaying, or denying far too long? Unfinished business filling you with a nagging sense of dread and unrest? Something you'd like to be done with once and for all?

> I create many of my dragons myself by simply putting off small tasks until they take on a life of their own, growing into something menacing and huge.

Maybe you're a procrastinator like I am. I create many of my dragons myself by simply putting off small tasks until they take on a life of their own, growing into something menacing and huge.

Sort of like the time I ended up with this warrant out for my arrest.

Midlife Mom Turned Hardened Criminal

It started simply enough. I was driving too fast. When the cop in the squad car behind me gave several quick chirps of his siren and turned on his lights, I grimaced and made my way to the shoulder of the highway.

I did a quick lipstick check and fluffed my hair although, to be honest, the pretty smile routine that got me out of numerous tickets in my teens and twenties stopped working a good fifteen years ago, a fact I find loathsome to admit.

Sure enough, he wrote me a ticket.

I was furious with myself. I hadn't gotten a ticket in half a dozen years, and now this! Even worse, the fine was a big one, more than a hundred bucks. None of which made it any easier when, two weeks later, on the exact same stretch of highway, I landed a SECOND speeding ticket, and this time the fine was even bigger.

I was disgusted. What a stupid waste of time and money this was going to turn out to be. I could attend traffic school for the first ticket, but I'd have to pay the fine on the second.

In fact, the whole incident was so incredibly distasteful to me that I promptly stashed it in the very back of a dark, crowded closet in the farthest corner of my mind.

It was still there when the traffic school deadline came and went.

It stayed there when I got a notice in the mail reminding me that the deadline for my fines was just around the corner.

It was still there when the letter arrived informing me that my fines were no longer due but overdue, and that I needed to act promptly to avoid further unpleasantries.

To be honest, the pretty smile routine that got me out of numerous tickets in my teens and twenties stopped working a good fifteen years ago.

And it was still there, moldering in the dark, when I received the memo casually informing me that a warrant had been issued for my arrest.

By now the whole mess was so incredibly painful to think about, I not only kept it in my mental closet but put a lock on the door as well. Every time it came to mind, I winced and thought, *I am such an idiot! I NEED to take care of that! What's wrong with me? I can't believe what a mess I've created! I'll definitely take care of this. As soon as I can bear to think about it. Like maybe next week.*

My friend Beth Forester was over one night when Larry announced the fact that I was a wanted woman. I had no choice but to unburden myself of the entire story. When I was done, Beth grabbed my purse and my arm and her car keys and began steering us toward the front door.

Larry said, "Where are you going? It's eleven o'clock at night."

Beth said, "To the jail."

I said, "Beth! *Et tu, Bruté?*"

She laughed. "Oh, not to turn you in. On the south side of the downtown jail there's a cashier's window. It's open 24/7 for situations just like this one. It's in a rather lively part of town, so you'll enjoy seeing the nightlife. Besides, I might not be home the day you use your one phone call to call someone to come bail you out. Then where would you be? I know black is slimming, but those horizontal stripes will NOT be a good look on you, trust me."

So that's how we ended up in a seedy part of downtown Dallas at one in the morning, carrying a thick envelope of unmarked bills. We cleared my name and celebrated with a cup of coffee at Denny's.

Case closed.

Well, almost closed. Just one little question remains to be answered.

Remind me to ask Beth how she knew about that window!

Lose the Loose Ends

There are days I feel burdened with this gnawing sense that all is not well in my life. Sometimes—like in the case of my speeding tickets—I can pinpoint the exact source of my discomfort.

But there are other days when the genesis of this boding feeling is something I can't quite finger. It's not until I finally slay my dragon—pay that overdue fine, make that phone call I've been putting off, meet my deadline, face that fear I've been denying, or have that tough conversation I've been delaying—that I realize how much fear and dread had been impacting my life.

Suddenly the shadow over my life is gone and the sun is shining again, the world a bright place filled with possibilities.

I'm sure you know what I'm talking about, that sense of relief and freedom that comes when you face something you've been dreading, deal with it, and move on with your life.

How can you and I enjoy that feeling more often? How can we keep lizard-like loose ends in our lives from evolving into dragonesque dilemmas? Here are some ideas.

Isolate Your Enemy

What's so hard to face about a speeding ticket?

Sure, it's unpleasant, but it's just a piece of paper. Okay, two pieces of paper that cost me several hundred dollars but hardly the end of the world. Why was it so hard for me to face?

I suspect that what I hated facing was not my tickets but the self-condemnation and shame I attached to my tickets. Together—unpleasant task PLUS painful emotions I attached to that task—they created a one-two punch that was hard to for me to deflect.

Just like last year. After discovering a small lump in one breast, it took me six months to make the phone call to arrange a mammogram (which was normal, by the way). Why? Is the mammogram so very horrible? Nah, just a little unpleasant. But when I added fear into the mix, I had a dragon on my hands. Once again, unpleasant task PLUS painful emotion became a dynamic duo that sent me fleeing the other direction.

We've all heard the saying "divide and conquer." Sometimes that's a good approach to conquering procrastination. Divide the task at hand from any unnecessary—perhaps even over-reactive—emotional baggage and see if the task doesn't suddenly become more manageable.

"This is just a ticket. This does NOT mean I am a failure as a citizen of the human race."

"This is merely a mammogram. This does NOT mean I should make an appointment with an estate planner."

You get the idea.

Herald the Cavalry

Last week I called my sister Michelle on the phone. As we chatted, I discovered that she was feeling as overwhelmed by her undone housework as I was by mine.

I said, "I'll help you. I'll come over and we'll spend several hours cleaning your house together."

She said, "Then next week I'll come to your house and we'll do the same."

Well, today was my day. Michelle drove to my house. We sat on my couch drinking coffee and planning our tasks for the day.

There's no question that my house needs help. Several pharmaceutical companies have offered to pay me handsomely so they could conduct bacterial field tests in my kitchen alone. I figure, at this rate, my bathrooms could probably put my kids through medical school.

But instead of handing Michelle the toilet bowl cleaner, I said, "There's something else I've been putting off for weeks. I could do it myself, but the fact is that I'm just not getting around to it, and you doing it with me would be a tremendous motivation."

I am not morally opposed to having a remote controlled dog. I push a button, he yelps and obeys. This works for me.

So we drove to PetSmart and bought a leather collar for my German shepherd, then took the leather collar to a shoe cobbler who punched holes in the leather, and then used those holes to attach a new battery pack and prongs so that Walter gets shocked every time he gets the notion to leave my fence-free backyard and run blindly into the path of any one of the four-thousand-pound SUVs that frequent the streets around my neighborhood.

Sounds simple, right? But for some reason, this task had turned into a dragon in my life. I don't know why. I am not morally opposed to having a remote controlled dog. I push a button, he yelps and obeys. This works for me. I figure it's

43

If I had acted two weeks ago, all I would have needed was a collar. Now I'm probably going to have to hire a dog therapist and a landscaper.

better than explaining to my children why the family dog is five-feet-by-five-feet-by-two-inches and has tire tread marks down his spine.

But for some reason, when Walter's old collar needed replacing, I got stymied. I wasn't sure whether to buy a leather or nylon collar. I didn't know where to find a cobbler's shop. I had writing deadlines. I ran out of time. I wasn't going to be in the right end of town. In the meantime, with his old collar on the blink, Walter had been confined to the house or a long lead. This had been going on for two weeks—long enough for Walter's anxious pacing to wear a muddy path in my backyard lawn. If I had acted two weeks ago, all I would have needed was a collar. Now I'm probably going to have to hire a dog therapist and a landscaper.

So you can see how this particular loose-end lizard had been morphing into a dragon before my very eyes.

The truth is, I needed help and I needed it fast, and it came in the form of someone coming alongside and saying, "Hey, let's do this together."

Tonight Walter is sporting his new collar and enjoying the freedom of a secure backyard.

And there's one less dragon breathing down my neck.

What about in your life? Do you have important projects that seem beyond your ability to complete? Things you should have done three weeks ago? Loose ends that nag at your peace of mind? Ask a friend to help you slay a few of the dragons that have taken up residence in your life and promise to return the favor by helping her kill a few of her own.

Carry a Fire Extinguisher

If you can't put a dragon in its grave, sometimes you can temporarily put out his fire.

Like the time I was really, really, really, really late on a book manuscript.

As you can imagine, the last person in the world I wanted to talk to was my editor. In fact, every time the phone rang I winced. Every morning when I opened my e-mails I expected to find one from her saying, "Maybe I should get one of those little boxes for MY social life, because ever since you got Caller ID you're never home!"

One night I even dreamed about her. I dreamed we ran into each other at a convention and she was still speaking to me. In fact, she even gave me a hug. I felt so relieved!

> If you can't put a dragon in its grave, sometimes you can temporarily put out his fire.

Then I woke up.

I hated living in dread. It would take me weeks to finish my manuscript and put this dragon six feet under ground. Imagine living this way for another month and a half!

But I wasn't helpless. If I couldn't completely extinguish my dragon, I could at least extinguish some of the heat I was feeling. I stopped avoiding the inevitable and picked up the phone.

I dialed Lonnie's number.

She said hello.

I said, "It's me."

She said, "Karen who?"

I said, "I know I'm a pain to work with. You've been gracious nevertheless. And guess what? I'm working fast and furious. You'll have everything in a couple weeks."

I don't remember what she said, but she was very happy. She might even have said she would hug me at the next convention.

See? Dreams *can* come true.

My point is this: My phone call didn't eliminate my deadline. But it sure turned down the heat.

Is there something you can do to extinguish some of the fire while you continue making efforts to eliminate the dragon?

Can you make a phone call, mail a payment, or write a letter? Can you refrain, detain, complain, or explain?

Hang in there. Dragons aren't always felled in a single blow. But that doesn't mean they're not going down.

Take a Chill Pill

You can't always keep things in your life from slipping through the cracks or spinning out of control.

But you can control how you respond.

Lose the Loose Ends

Are you being held hostage by loose ends in your life? Try these suggestions to cut the ties that bind and gag:

◎ Ask for help. Recruit a friend, relative, professional housekeeper, bookkeeper, or neighborhood kid to help you with a few of the more stubborn projects that have been dogging you for months.

◎ Don't let the tyranny of the urgent rule your life twenty-four hours a day! Instead, allot time every day for these three things: (1) urgent tasks, (2) long-term projects (a little attention today will keep them from turning into dragons tomorrow) and (3) a little dreaming about the future to keep you energized and inspired.

◎ Try to handle each bill, task, e-mail, snail mail, or piece of paper as it comes into your life rather than merely glancing at it and hoarding it in a stack to handle later.

◎ Keep a running list of things you need to do and work from that list—don't rely on your memory!

Besides, some loose ends are necessary. They are the natural thread between our yesterdays and tomorrows. They mean you have a history and a future. Indeed, yesterday's unfinished business provides the strands we need to begin weaving our lives today.

Loose ends don't mean we're failures. They mean we're alive.

So the next time your life feels overrun by loose-end lizards, fire-breathing dragons, or even a stucco-clinging spider, take a deep breath. Then pick up the phone and give me a call.

I'll send Larry right over.

4

Move to a New State of Mind

A lot can happen in six weeks.

Six weeks ago we were vacationing at my parents' home in Colorado Springs when Larry had the opportunity to interview for a position at a university just outside of Denver. A week later he was offered the job. After much prayerful consideration, he accepted.

The good news is that once we moved, I would be within "meet me for lunch" distance from my family.

The bad news is that we had exactly three weeks to return to Texas, sell our home, pack up our belongings, and move to Colorado.

When we broke the news to Kaitlyn and Kacie, we got mixed reviews.

Kaitlyn, fourteen, said, "I don't want to move and leave all my friends in Texas. But I've had a feeling that God was going to lead us here, so I'm just going to trust him. I guess I can't look back. And the future's unseen so I can't really look forward. I guess my only option is to look up."

My lower jaw must have been hanging somewhere in the vicinity of my kneecap. It's always amazing and humbling when you see spiritual maturity in your kids. I'm not sure where she gets it. Must be from her dad.

Six-year-old Kacie took a decidedly less spiritual approach.

She said, "I hate the mountains."

I said, "Excuse me?"

She said, "I HATE the mountains. They're EVERY-WHERE here. They're in front of me. They're behind me. They're side to side."

I said, "I think they're beautiful! Why do you hate them?"

She tossed her head. "They remind me I don't belong here, because I'm a NATIVE Texan and in Texas we don't HAVE mountains."

I could see this was going to be a problem.

I said, "Kacie, how can I make this a more pleasant experience for you?"

She thought a few moments before giving me her answer. When she finally spoke, this is what she said:

She requested the down payment of one Barbie to be purchased that very day, with the balance of ten Barbies to be purchased in three weeks when we completed our move.

It was an eleven-Barbie relocation package.

We shook hands to seal the deal.

I knew my girls would have many adjustments to make, but I could see they were going to be okay. I decided to turn my attention to the move itself. It was time to look at my life and decide what to take with me to Colorado and what to leave behind.

Household goods were the least of my concern.

A Fresh Start

The past several years have been interesting ones for me. If you read my last book—*Sometimes I Wake Up Grumpy . . . and Sometimes I Let Him Sleep*—you know part of the story. For seventeen years, Larry and I worked hard to ignore some serious flaws in the foundation of our relationship. Putting many of my emotions on hold, I managed to get by until three years ago when I woke up one morning overwhelmed by loss and anger and pain. It was as though a dam had burst inside of me and raging currents of emotion flooded my world. Feeling hurt and angry and rebellious, I faced temptations and depression. My faith took a beating, and my marriage was stressed and redefined nearly beyond what we could bear.

Looking back from where I stand today, I can see that I was, among other things, grieving fiercely. Experts say there are five stages of grief, and I became intimately acquainted with four of them as I ricocheted between denial, anger, depression, and "If only. . ." regrets and wishes. I had come through the worst of it when I began to write *Grumpy*, but my healing was far from complete.

> It's possible that, like me, you're ready to move to a new and improved state of emotional wellness.

I'm still healing. But in the past twelve months I've experienced breakthroughs of well-being and rekindlings of joy. I've explored new perspectives about my relationship with myself and with God. They say the fifth stage of grief is acceptance. I'm wondering if that's where I'm at. I think it might be, because I'm finally getting to the place where the old hurts are losing some of their power, and what I'd really like most of all is to get on with my life.

Maybe that's what this move means to me. A new beginning. A chance for my marriage to revive, survive, and maybe, eventually, to thrive. A time to put away the old and embrace the new. We'll see. I'll keep you updated. But in the meantime, the whole thing's got me thinking about moving on, and I'm wondering about YOU. It's possible that, like me, you're ready to move to a new state. Not a different state of the Union but a new and improved state of emotional wellness.

When we've been hurt, when we've grieved, when we've raged and wallowed and whined, what then? As we survey our lives in anticipation of a change of address or change of heart, can we pack the best and discard the rest?

I think we can. I'm still figuring out how to do it in my life, but here's what I've learned so far.

Give Yourself Permission to Feel Good

Several months ago I began walking again after a year-long hiatus from exercise. As I dusted off my Reeboks and Walkman cassette player, I knew I'd been away from healthy living too long.

A week or two later, I had the most marvelous experience.

I was about thirty minutes into my walk, really pumping to the music, when I looked up and saw two squirrels chasing each other along a picket fence. Nothing all that amazing, but their antics made me laugh out loud. I really got a kick out of those squirrels. With a small start of surprise, I realized it had been a while since I'd felt those little bubbles in my spirit. I recognized them for what they were—joy—and kept on walking, now with a smile on my face.

About ten minutes later I turned down another street when suddenly I raised my nose in the air. What was that heavenly smell? Ah, yes. Honeysuckle! The fragrance hung with me for about half a block, and I enjoyed every moment. My face raised to the sun, the scent of honeysuckle filling my senses, another familiar emotion flooded my soul. It took me a few moments to fully recognize it: gratitude.

A little farther and I passed a woman getting out of a car with a small child. We didn't know each other, but she smiled at me, flashed a raised thumb, and hollered, "Way to go! Keep it up!" and I surged forward, buoyed by new inspiration.

By then I was almost home. As I walked the final blocks, I embraced the good feelings I had just experienced and hung on tight. *Joy. Gratitude. Inspiration.* Wow! What a rush!

A few years ago when I was really hurting, most of my days had been fueled by angst as I gave myself permission to embrace my pain and grieve without reservation. Whenever a good feeling happened to come my way, I barely acknowledged it. Like a loyal lover, I was too committed to my pain to embrace anything else.

But on my heart-opening walk, for the first time in a long time I gave myself permission to feel good. Not just good, but even great. Joy. Gratitude. Inspiration. This time I invited them to stay. As I approached my front porch, I breathed deeply, satisfied and content.

It was good to be home again.

Having a Joyful Moment? Share the Good News

Several weeks later I was driving in the car with my daughters and two of their friends. I had just picked everyone up from school and we were heading to my house when suddenly I had a great idea. I grinned and pulled a U-turn.

"Where are we going?" Kaitlyn asked.

I said, "To the movies!"

I drove on, my car filled with the happy chatter of girls, and I felt great. I felt footloose. I felt like a summer day. I felt, well, happy.

The next day I called my sister. When she answered the phone I blurted, "I had a great day yesterday! I felt HAPPY!"

She smiled at me, flashed a raised thumb, and hollered, "Way to go! Keep it up!"

She said, "Wow! Well, okay. That's great!!"

I explained, "You know, in the past several years I've called you a hundred times when I've been hurting, when I've been in tears, when I've felt depressed or overwhelmed. And then yesterday I had this really great day. I just had fun. I was happy. And I figured you deserved to hear that kind of news as well."

I don't know why I hit such a wall a few years ago. Relationship issues, midlife crisis, spiritual warfare, clinical depression, the inevitable crash-and-burn of long-term denial, whatever. I'm still figuring it out.

Increasingly in recent months I've started to experience joy again. But in the midst of my ongoing healing, there have been times when I've (this is not easy to admit) had this unsettling urge to (I know this sounds crazy) keep my good feelings under wrap.

> Are we willing to put down our sack of sorrows long enough to embrace something better?

Partly I was afraid my returning joy was fleeting. Like a spooked kitten regaining her courage, my joy seemed to be cautiously nosing its way back to my outstretched palm, but I couldn't say for sure it wouldn't startle and bolt once again.

So that was one reason for my hesitation.

The other reason is far less noble. In fact, it's sort of embarrassing to admit, but here it is: There have been days I've wanted to keep my returning joy a secret because, well, I wasn't sure what people would think.

I've actually found myself thinking, *I'd better not tell anyone. If they know I'm feeling better they'll think, "Oh, well, see? Everything's fine after all. She sure made a fuss about nothing."* Indeed, a few times lately when friends have asked, "So how are you?" I've sidestepped the question, hiding my healing because I didn't want my newfound joy to somehow diminish the validity and depth of whatever it was I'd just gone through.

Other times I've fought that urge and won. The day I called my sister was one of the winning days.

When we've experienced a great deal of emotional pain, are we willing to put down our sack of sorrows long enough to embrace something better, and then are we courageous enough to tell the folks around us that we're moving on?

Sometimes I think when we've lived somewhere a very long time, it's possible to become "defined" in some way by our address. In Texas, I lived for a long time in a beautiful raised cottage with a sweeping front porch straight from the pages of *Southern Living*. I entertained a lot in that house. Most of my friends knew my house nearly as well as their own. It had a big kitchen where I cooked up a mess of green beans and brisket for company more times than I can shake a stick at, and a claw-foot kitchen table where we drank Dr Pepper and coffee, played Sequence, and talked for hours, solving the world's problems and sometimes even our own. I know that when many of my friends think of me, that white-porched house on Fairlawn Drive will probably come to mind as well, at least for some time to come.

Sooner or later, they'll all see me in my new home, and by the second or third visit, when they think of Karen Linamen, the image that will come to mind won't be Karen serving brisket in her Texas cottage but Karen drinking coffee on the deck of her hill-hugging Colorado ranch home with the killer front-range view.

And that's okay.

Sometimes change is just what the doctor ordered.

What about you? Are you ready to move to a new state of well-being? Are you ready for a change of heart? Give yourself permission to feel good, then don't hesitate to tell your friends and family about milestones in your journey back to joy. Just because you're finally getting over a long-standing grudge or wound or failure doesn't trivialize the pain you suffered. It simply means that it's time to move on, and I'm guessing that most of your friends—the true ones, at least—will be thrilled to hear the news.

Budge a Grudge with Gratitude

Any move requires a little housecleaning. I can't tell you how much I dreaded sorting out all the boxes and junk that had accumulated in the two attics of my house in Texas.

It was amazing all the stuff that was up there. Stuff I didn't need. Stuff that was taking up valuable space and collecting dust, dust mites, and mouse droppings in the process.

Some of it was hard to move. Heavy boxes filled to the brim, pieces of broken furniture, cartons of old files and paperwork. Some days I wished I had a crane. Or a bulldozer. Or maybe just a lengthy visit from a dozen of the beefy weightlifters who frequent my gym.

Moving to a new state of being? You might have some stuff that needs to be relocated to the dump, and if it's very heavy at all you might need a hand budging it in the process.

Antique grudge? Historical hurt? Painful memories? Dusty lusts? Why lug it with you?

As I began to heal, gratitude became increasingly possible.

In reality, you don't need a half-dozen hunky weightlifters (I know you're disappointed). Budging that grudge, bad habit, or memory requires a different kind of muscle.

What kind of muscle? How about gratitude? There's a muscle that'll work hard for you. Now, I agree, when we're REALLY hurting, it's hard to feel grateful for anything. But what I found in my life was that as I began to heal, gratitude became increasingly possible. Like any muscle that hadn't been used for a while, it started off rather puny and weak, but I'm finding that the more I exercise it, the stronger it's becoming.

How do I know my gratitude muscle is getting stronger? A week ago I wrote a letter to a dear friend of mine. I'll admit that, in my note, I whined a little—not a lot, just a little—about some current challenges. But here's what I said at the end:

> I do know that suddenly I'm living in one of the most beautiful spots on the face of the earth, in a wonderful house, driving my dream car, and raising the two most incredible kids in the universe. Two days ago we attended Jubilee Fellowship in Littleton, a church I picked out, and everyone loved it, so it looks like we'll be going back again next week. We've been here three weeks and already had two family gatherings celebrating the birthdays of my sister and brother-in-law, the kind of memory-making I've missed out on for ten years, and I loved

every minute of it. Walter has become a great car-traveler and goes with us in the back of my 4Runner every time we spend an evening at my folks' (which gives him a place to run, and also keeps him safe from the bears and mountain lions—lots of bear sightings around this whole area this month! Very interesting!).

So there are many things to be grateful for. I don't think I was in a frame of mind or spirit to feel grateful about ANY-THING when I first met you, do you agree?

And I wasn't. I was in a lot of pain, and my gratitude muscle was atrophied nearly beyond recognition. But I'm trying to build it up, work it regularly, and as I do, I'm finding that it's more and more capable of muscling those old grudges and habits and hurts out of the way.

How's that old hymn go? "Count your blessings, name them one by one, and it will surprise you what the Lord has done."

So get buff. Start counting. Hefting those dusty, nasty discards may be a lot easier than you think.

And once your move is underway—as you begin to pack the attitudes you want to keep (like joy, gratitude, and inspiration), and toss the attitudes you don't (those antique grudges come to mind)—do something nice for yourself. Maybe buy yourself a little gift. Something to celebrate the changes occurring in your life.

Eleven Barbies come to mind.

5

· ·

Cinematherapy, Anyone?

I remember the first time I made an intentional effort to use a movie as a mood-altering substance.

My husband and I were newlyweds living in Indiana while he pursued his doctorate. Indeed, Larry's days were grueling affairs as he worked full time, attended classes, appeased his doctoral committee, and slaved over his dissertation. To make matters worse, we were living on a shoestring budget. The most difficult adjustment came when Larry's mother was diagnosed with cancer.

To say that my husband frequently felt stressed and overwhelmed would be an understatement.

One Friday he was particularly down, and I racked my brain to think of something that would lift his spirits.

The obvious things came to mind: sex, food, cutting up my credit cards. Suddenly I decided, nah, I wanted something different. Something innovative. Something he'd never expect.

I decided to take him to the movies.

It was perfect! Two hours of distraction. Something that would help him relax. Lift his spirits. Reduce his stress. Lower his blood pressure. Transport him into a more positive frame of mind. I remembered the name of a movie he'd said he wanted to see. It was something I'd never heard of, but I was willing to watch anything that might help. At the box office, I plunked down my money, then steered Larry into the darkened theater. He went willingly.

Not unlike a lamb to slaughter.

I say this because the movie was entitled *The Thing*.

I racked my brain to think of something that would lift his spirits. I decided to take him to the movies.

Let me just say that it was the most alien-infested, gut-exploding, blood-spattering, gore-riddled, adrenaline-charging, pulse-pumping, tic-inducing, stress-producing flick I had seen in my twenty-two years on earth.

By the time we left the theater, we were quivering masses of adrenaline. We had spent so much time on the edge of our seats, the backs of our thighs were creased. Between the nervous tic in his cheek and his white knuckles, Larry looked like Humphrey Bogart at Coney Island.

So much for stress reduction.

Getting audited by the IRS would have been less stressful. Substituting for an air traffic controller would have been less stressful. Spending forty-seven days in a tie for the office of president of the United States would have been less stressful than sitting through two hours of *The Thing*.

I'm glad to say that, as abysmal as the experiment turned out to be, it didn't ruin me forever on the idea of using movies to lift my spirits. In fact, out of my utter commitment to you, dear reader, I've devoted many hours in the past two decades conducting extensive research on this very subject. This research has consisted of going to movies and renting videos—not to mention consuming popcorn and Milk Duds—and saving all my receipts for tax deductions just in case I ever wrote anything about movies in any of my books.

Which, now that I'm doing it, makes me a lot less vulnerable should a tax audit ever come my way.

See? My spirits feel lifted already.

"One Large Popcorn, Extra Butter, Please"

What is it about watching a movie that can transport you not only into a different world and time but also into a new frame of mind? For a couple of hours, your problems and circumstances are miles away as you immerse yourself in the fantasy world created by Hollywood's magicians. Even when the credits have finished flickering across the screen, the mood lingers, doesn't it? It's as though movies have attitudes, and those attitudes are contagious.

Is this a long-term fix? Nah. But for a little short-term relief, movies can make us laugh, help us cry, inspire our spirits, or just make us grateful that—unlike the idiot in a slasher movie who descends creaky stairs into a darkened basement while waving a flashlight and saying, "Honey? Is that you?"—you and I are still alive and well.

> For a little short-term relief, movies can make us laugh, help us cry, inspire our spirits, or just make us grateful that we are still alive and well.

Not that movies can't have a long-term impact. My brother-in-law Harald was an engineer before he joined the Navy for an eight-year stint as a fighter pilot. Why did he switch? He claims he watched *Top Gun* one too many times. My sister Renee says, "Don't laugh. He's not joking."

We know movies can influence, if not our actions, our attitudes and values. This is what fuels the debate over the impact of movie violence on society. This is why we guard what we let our kids watch.

So why not use movie impact for good? Why not keep a library of favorites that massage our emotions toward joy or courage or gratitude or greatness? Look, an hour of psychotherapy costs a hundred bucks, while two hours of cinematherapy can be had for a video rental and some microwave popcorn. Now, I have to admit that sometimes I've struggled in such a fashion that professional counseling was called for, and in those moments not even Mel Gibson could have helped. But there have been plenty of other moments when life's dilemmas weren't so crushing and two hours of cinema magic left me feeling better than I did before.

Better Living through the World of Make-Believe

When I was growing up, a lot of people put going to movies on the same list as dancing and chewing gum in church—it might not keep you out of heaven, but why take the chance?

An hour of psychotherapy costs a hundred bucks, while two hours of cinematherapy can be had for a video rental and some microwave popcorn.

In fact, my parents banned movie-going for most of my childhood. I was fourteen before they gave in and took my sisters and me to see our first movie. The year was 1974, and the movie was *Return of the Pink Panther* with Peter Sellers. We hummed da dum, da dum, dadum-dadum-dadum-dadum-dadum . . . da da da dum for several years, as I recall.

Our second movie was *The Apple Dumpling Gang* with Bill Bixby. This was before Bill got famous playing the Incredible Hulk, a creature who was seriously into bodybuilding until he apparently got gangrene all over his body from a small cut received at the hand of the careless barber who had just given him the worst haircut of his life. After that, he didn't go to the gym as much, as most of his time was spent accidentally terrorizing entire communities while feeling hormonal and misunderstood, not unlike many teenagers today.

Thirty years ago, my family and others may have been slow to embrace the magic of the big screen, but other families weren't so hesitant. To this day, Lonnie is passionate about cinema because of the sanity-saving role that movies played in her life as child. She remembers, "My parents were the only divorced people I knew, and on my weekends with my dad, he didn't know what to do with me. As a result, I went to movies all weekend. Matinees, by myself, center section, eight rows from the front.

"I saw a lot of Disney movies—*Cinderella, Bambi, Sleeping Beauty*—westerns and spy movies too. The stories fed my imagination. I used to wander up and down the ornate hallways of the lavish Michigan Theater in Jackson pretending I was a spy. The first time I went to a movie there, my dad took me, and I was so small I got to stand on the seat. They've restored that theater, and it brings me to tears to go there. I credit movies for keeping my childhood fairly sane. Videos are nice. But movie theaters are magic. And the popcorn is not optional."

> Most of us have taken movie-going (and even gum-chewing) off the no-no list.

Forty years later, Lonnie says that when she needs a moment's respite from the stresses of life, she returns to the cinema. She goes to matinees by herself. She sits center section, eight rows from the front. And the popcorn is mandatory.

As for me, I still smile whenever I hear that unmistakable Pink Panther theme music.

Yeah, movies definitely have feel-good power. And since most of us have taken movie-going (and even gum-chewing) off the no-no list, why not make good use of it? Best yet, now that we all have VCRs and DVDs, all that feel-goodness can be had for the price of a movie rental, unlike an experience I had nearly two decades ago, when the quest to watch a rented video nearly cost me my life, not to mention several thousand dollars in auto body work. The incident to which I'm referring occurred shortly after *The Alien* fiasco, where I encouraged Larry to lower his blood pressure by watching ravenous extraterrestrials slash and slaughter a small community of Arctic researchers (thus lowering the blood pressure of each researcher immeasurably).

It all started late one Thursday when the local weatherman advised the cancellation of work and school for the rest of the week, as we were merely hours from experiencing the worst blizzard in the history of our little town.

Naturally, this made us call friends and want to throw a party. Greg and Cheryl Heberling were, like us, newly married and sans children, and as long as we were all going to be snowed in, we figured we might as well be snowed in together.

Cheryl made a huge pot of chili. Greg rented several videos. We and several other friends drove to their home and crossed our fingers.

By morning the snow was so high it had completely covered the windows on one side of the house, casting an eerie white-green light on everything inside. We chuckled at our good fortune as we threw more logs into the Heberlings' wood-burning stove and drank cider in our stockinged feet. The chili and videos called our names.

That's when Greg remembered that we didn't have the VCR. It was across town at a friend's house.

There was way too much snow for us to drive home.

There was way too much snow for us to drive to work.

But there was NOT too much snow for seven of us to sardine ourselves into Larry's Honda Civic and slide, skid, and spin seven miles on rural roads to retrieve the VCR.

At one point we got stuck in a snowdrift, and the five guys piled out of the front and back seats and pushed us back onto the road. I remember watching them through the glass of the

> There was way too much snow for us to drive home. There was way too much snow for us to drive to work. But there was NOT too much snow for us to slide, skid, and spin seven miles on rural roads to retrieve the VCR.

64

back window since Cheryl and I had been stuffed in the hatch-back compartment and, even if we could have gotten out, the odds of us finding the right combination of yoga contortions that would have allowed us to return to our allotted space—which was bigger than a milk carton but smaller than a microwave—seemed unlikely.

But the rewards of our risk-taking were sweet.

We not only made it home alive, no one lost a single body part due to frostbite or even lack of circulation. Best yet, we watched our favorite movies until dawn.

Take Two Raisinets and Call Me in the Morning

Whether you prefer watching movies in a theater or in the comfort of your own home, there's no denying that movies can comfort, inspire, educate, inform, entertain, and uplift.

In our quest to manage, alleviate, and even enjoy the insanity in our lives, let's not overlook the potential of a well-placed movie now and then, shall we? Not sure what movie will do the trick? Ask friends for recommendations. Look up your favorite actors on the Internet, check out their filmographies, and catch up on any movies you might have missed. And the next time you rent a flick, don't forget to check out the classic movie section.

You can even do like I did and make yourself a 911 list of your favorite flicks as antidotes for a variety of emotional crises. For example, when I'm feeling blue, nothing cheers me better than watching Goldie Hawn and Kurt Russell seek revenge—and find love instead—in their movie *Overboard*.

When it's me against the odds, I love watching Michael Keaton gain victory over spit-up, laundry, temptation, and an expanding waistline in *Mr. Mom*. Diane Keaton triumphs as she balances motherhood and career in *Baby Boom*. And inspiring favorites about young people who pursue impossible dreams include *Rudy, Iron Will,* and *Wild Hearts Can't Be Broken*.

When I just want to feel good all over, nothing beats a romantic comedy. One of my personal favorites is *Runaway Bride* with Gere and Roberts. I also love children's-literature-with-a-twist stories, such as *Hook, The Princess Bride,* and *Ever After.* Other movies good for a general lift? How about all those Doris Day classics we loved as teenagers? And *The Parent Trap* featuring Haley Mills (and Haley Mills) is as fun now as it was when we were twelve.

Of course, when I want to feel grateful that I'm alive, I watch *Twister, Independence Day,* and *Jaws* (just not in the same evening unless I take my blood pressure medicine). And when I'm in the mood for a good cry, it's gotta be *Cyrano de Bergerac* with Gérard Depardieu.

For Medicinal Purposes Only

Next time one of your friends comes down with the blues or the flu, treat her to a movie—for medicinal purposes, naturally. Take her a gift basket or decorative box—or, if you are as un-Martha-Stewartesque as I am, a shopping bag—filled with the following:

- ◎ Several rented movies (consider retrieving the movies in a few days so you don't saddle your flu-ridden friend with the responsibility of returning them!)
- ◎ Several bags of microwave popcorn
- ◎ Some typical movie candy—Twizzlers, Raisinets, or Milk Duds come to mind!
- ◎ A box of Kleenex
- ◎ A two-liter bottle of her favorite soda
- ◎ A plastic cup and straw from your local movie theater (It won't hurt to stop by and ask theater management to contribute to your cause ...the worst they can do is say no!)

So there you have it, my brand of cinematherapy for when life feels crazy and I need to laugh, cry, cheer up, buck up, straighten up, or count my blessings.

But this is what works for me. My guess is that you have your own favorite mood-altering flicks. If so, I'd love to hear about them! E-mail me at thefunnyfarm@email.com and share your cinematherapy strategies, and perhaps I'll include some of the suggestions I receive in my next book.

Bottom line, sometimes a quick fix isn't such a bad thing. So grab a snack, commandeer the remote, turn down the lights, and let the good times roll!

6

....

Get a New Boditude

Forget bad hair day. I was having a bad body decade.

How do you know you're having a bad body decade?

When you can't cross your legs under a table.

When "one size fits all" applies to everybody but you.

When you catch a surprise glimpse of yourself in a mirror and think, *Thank goodness I don't look as bad as HER!*

I was so embarrassed by my body, I was always trying to figure ways to make love to my husband without actually getting naked. Dark rooms helped some, but I felt most comfortable hiding behind several layers of clothing. If I could have made love to him from another room, I would have. I suggested phone sex once, but it didn't work out well for us. I called him at his office. When he said, "Where are you and what are you wearing?" I said, "I'm standing in a dark room wearing three sweat suits and a coat." It didn't turn him on. Go figure.

Eventually I got so fed up I lost sixty pounds. I did what they've been telling us to do for years: I exercised and ate healthy. Who knew?

What I also did—and continue to do—is work on my boditude.

Look, the numbers on a scale are one thing. But they're not the only thing. I've met plenty of thin women who feel insecure and unlovable. I've met large women who exude confidence and sensuality. You probably have too.

That's what I mean by boditude.

The truth is, losing weight is great. But there are countless other things you and I can do that will enable us to feel sexy, feminine, whole, strong, healthy, confident, pretty, and desirable—at any weight, size, or shape we might happen to be.

> I've met plenty of thin women who feel insecure and unloveable. I've met large women who exude confidence and sensuality. That's boditude.

My Personal Turning Point

I remember whining to my sister Michelle, "I'll never be pretty again."

The truth is, I had let myself go in every way imaginable. I'd gained 120 unwanted pounds, and I wasn't even putting forth minimal effort in the hair, skin, makeup, or jewelry departments. Lingerie? I figured that was something skinny girls wore. I settled for old ladies' panties from Kmart.

I'd tried diets before, but nothing seemed to work long-term.

What finally helped me turn a corner? It's hard to say. Perhaps there were two things. The first is a little unorthodox, but it happened, and so here it is—somebody flirted with me, and that simple act reminded me of something I'd long forgotten. It reminded me what it felt like to be a woman again, confident, attractive, and feminine.

One other thing happened. I had one of those horrible moments I've already described; you know, the kind where you walk past a window or mirror, catch a surprise glimpse of yourself, and think, *Thank goodness I don't look as bad as THAT!* and then you realize that, well, actually, you do.

Perhaps there was a third thing, and it had to do with deciding to come out of my cocoon. For years I'd lived in a cocoon of denial about some painful patterns in my marriage and I was finally ready to face the fact that something wasn't working. Maybe shedding my cocoon of denial enabled me to begin to shed my cocoon of pounds. All I know is that, all of a sudden, living numbed-out—by denial or pounds—didn't seem like such a good idea anymore.

AWOL No Longer

I'd been AWOL—absent without leave—for a lot of years. Best as I can tell, that's exactly what was occurring as I numbed myself with denial and with food—I was AWOL from my life and from my body. I can picture a shell-shocked soldier crawling under the wire and sprinting for home. I was sprinting from my life too—and abusing the truth and abusing food helped me to do it.

I figured I'd been absent long enough. It was time to show up and reclaim my body and my life. And the first place I decided to show up was the gym.

In the beginning, I had no other goal than to dress in my sweats, drive to the gym, and stand on the treadmill. Five days a week. If I felt like walking, great; if not, fine, I could go home knowing that I'd met my goal for the day.

I walked more days than not.

It felt good, just getting my internal organs moving. My heart and lungs and muscles protested at first, but before long they were thanking me. Outside, I was still fat. But my innards were getting sexier every day. No doubt if I'd needed surgery, any red-blooded American doctor would have opened me up

> It was time to show up and reclaim my body and my life. And the first place I decided to show up was the gym.

71

and fallen in love with me on the spot. Not to mention the fact that by now I could walk from the couch to the refrigerator without getting winded.

On the outside, my body still looked the same. But inside, a new body attitude—not unlike the beginnings of a very shy smile—began to stir.

By now I could walk from the couch to the refrigerator without getting winded.

I decided I needed some color. Steering clear of the bronzed-skin-cancer-candidate motif, I experimented with sunless tanning lotions and visited a tanning bed once or twice a week. Pretty soon my skin no longer boasted a color most frequently viewed on the soft underbelly of a frog. My boditude grew from a Mona Lisa smile into something broader, something sporting a twinkle.

One day I took a good look into my underwear drawer. This can be scary if the last time you bought real lingerie was back when *Moonlighting* was on prime time.

I decided my unmentionables needed triage, and they needed it fast.

First I axed any pair of panties with more than the standard three holes. I also tossed panties I had retrieved from the rag bag, or bras with just one remaining underwire. Panties and bras with no discernable partners were also routed out of my drawer. No longer would I settle for a pair of leopard print panties worn with a navy blue bra. In a blinding flash of insight, I knew I needed *coordinating* underwear, and I needed it fast!

I began my shopping CPR anywhere I could find attractive lingerie in big-gal sizes. Even though I continued going to the gym, the truth is that my body wasn't changing nearly as fast as my body *attitude*.

Still, changes were occurring, and pretty soon I was able to order sexy things from the Victoria's Secret catalog. At first I was limited to lingerie offered in XL or D, but as I continued to work out, my options grew.

One day I was standing in the women's locker room in my skivvies, blow-drying my hair, when a woman approached me. I noticed right away that, although she was blond and thin, she did *not* have matching underwear.

She said, "We've met before," and reintroduced herself as the mom of one of Kacie's little playmates. Then she said, "You're wearing such beautiful underthings! And they match! What a wonderful idea! Under *my* clothes, I always look like I shop at the Salvation Army."

I've always envied women who can take a compliment with a certain savoir faire, who patiently murmur "Thank you" as if they are being kind to you because they have received that particular compliment upwards of a thousand times, women who can keep a secret, women who don't respond to a compliment by launching into their life story.

In a blinding flash of insight, I knew I needed *coordinating* underwear, and I needed it fast!

I envy these women because I am not one of them.

I gushed, "Dream Angels demi-bra and high-cut brief in Whisper Pink, Victoria's Secret catalog, page 112, winter clearance!"

She said, "Great tip! I'll check it out."

I ran into her at a neighborhood birthday party a few months later. She flashed a thumbs up sign and, when no one was looking, confided beamishly, "I *match!*"

Had I lost tons of weight? No way. Had my boditude grown from a tight-lipped frown into a genuine grin? You bet.

But I wanted more.

I wanted to laugh.

Belly laugh, to be exact.

Hello, Lyle

I remember the morning over breakfast when I told three of my closest friends that I wanted to get my belly button pierced.

Nancy said, "You're kidding, right?"

I said, "No, I am definitely not giving birth to a baby goat."

Darla said, "If you're going to do this, at least go to a clean establishment."

Cherie said, "No beer-bellied tattoo artists wearing leather and a bandana."

It sounded reasonable to me.

As soon as I got home I grabbed the Yellow Pages and located a tattoo parlor on Main Street in my little town.

I lived in Duncanville, Texas, at the time. Hardly Sin City. Sure enough, I dialed the number, and a very normal sounding man answered the phone. He had a nice white-collar voice. I mean, he could have been my dentist.

We introduced ourselves. He said his name was Lyle.

I said, "Tell me, Lyle, do you do belly button piercings?"

He said, "Certainly, we do that."

I said, "Do you do belly button piercings for forty-year-old women having a midlife crisis?"

He laughed and said, "Why, that happens to be our specialty!"

I said, "You sound like a very normal person. Is your establishment clean?"

He assured me that it was and described in detail how everything comes in sterilized packages, how he always wears gloves, yadda yadda yadda.

By then I was feeling really comfortable. All the sleazy tattoo parlor images were gone from my head. I mean, here's a normal guy, probably wearing Dockers and a collared shirt, in a little office not unlike my dentist's office, with berber carpet and turquoise Formica on the counters. So I'm cool. I'm fine. This is going to be fun.

I made my appointment for the following morning.

My friends Beth and Cherie offered to accompany me. At the last minute, Beth injured her back and Cherie was running late, so I drove to my appointment alone. Which didn't worry me, what with Lyle being such an Eddie Bauer sort of guy and all.

I drove to Main Street, parked my car, walked across the sidewalk, and opened the door to Lyle's place of business.

I said, "Lyle."

He said, "Karen."

And there he stood. Leather pants, full beard, bandana on his head, and tattoos covering every inch of his beefy arms, one of which he extended so I could shake his hand.

As I did, I looked around the shop. Images of berber carpeting and turquoise Formica fled in the face of reality, which included posters of snakes and motorcycles, display cases filled with chains, and racks of black T-shirts sporting reassuring phrases like "Why torture yourself? Let me do it instead."

I'll spare you the rest. Let me just say that I went through with it, Cherie by my side (she arrived just in time, although if you ask her, she'll say she came too late to achieve her goal, which I realize now was to talk some sense into my head).

I wore the ring for a year and loved every minute of it.

Did I flaunt it? Nope. It was for me. For smiles. For fun. It was a friendship ring, of sorts, to celebrate the fact that, for the first time in a decade, my body and I were happy to be together.

Your Turn

What do you need in order to improve *your* boditude? I've told you what worked for me. Your list may be different than mine, but rest assured that making friends with your body— not to mention feeling confident and sensual too—is within your grasp regardless of the numbers on your scale or the size of your hips.

Best yet, improving your body attitude doesn't have to cost an arm and a leg. Here are some ideas that are cost effective as well as fun:

◎ **Go cheapskate on some beauty strategies so you can splurge on others.** For example, I get $10 haircuts at Supercuts so I can afford acrylic nails. I buy $3 lip gloss but splurge on $14 Estee Lauder mascara.

◎ **Swap secrets with girlfriends.** My friend Linda got me turned on to a great haircolor I buy at my supermarket . . . Debbie told me about Ponds Age Defying Face Cream from Wal-Mart . . . Beth showed me how to bleach the hair on my arms and introduced me to a good electrologist in town.

As I love my body at every shape and size, I am teaching my daughters that the worth and beauty of a human being doesn't fluctuate with the numbers on a scale or the girth of a waistline.

◎ **Find a cheap thrill.** I love the way a really jazzy pair of sunglasses makes me feel. I always buy cheap glasses so I can afford to own several pairs—at ten bucks a pop, my collection of sunglasses is a little luxury that makes me feel on top of the world!

◎ **Other feel-better strategies that don't cost a dime?** Stay away from sodas and coffee and drink lots of water instead. Get plenty of sleep. Stand up straight for better posture. And perhaps the most effective body attitude secret of all—smile!

If you're still not convinced, think of what the people you love the most will gain from your new boditude. Daily, my girls reap the benefits of a healthier, more confident mother. As I take care of myself and love my body at every shape and size, I am teaching my daughters that the worth and beauty of a human being doesn't fluctuate with the numbers on a scale or the girth of a waistline. And when it comes to my love life . . . well, let me just say that I no longer make my husband turn out the lights and wait for a lunar eclipse before I get undressed.

Am I skinnie-minnie? No way. I'm still waiting for the day when I'll weigh less than my refrigerator. But the truth is, I like my body. We're friends. Three years ago when I thought about my body I felt sad. Today, with a brand-new body attitude, I'm able to smile, grin, and giggle.

I've even been known to belly laugh now and then.

7

....

Embrace the Here and Now

There are lots of maladies common to women.

I got an e-mail the other day from a reader who wrote, "I loved your story about keeping your tweezers in the car and plucking chin hairs at stop lights. I thought I was the only woman who did that! I also use my mascara to cover up my gray roots between hair colorings. But don't let it smudge. It's a mess!"

See? That's one of the things I love about being a woman. We may share common maladies, but we're also willing to share a good solution when we find one.

Last week I took Kacie to the park near my house. While she tackled the rope ladder, I introduced myself to a couple other moms there with their kids.

Within five minutes we were exchanging bladder control stories.

Honestly, I don't know how I get myself into these kinds of conversations with women I've known all of seven minutes, but this is not an unusual experience for me.

We blamed our pregnancies, of course, and then traded secrets about Kegels and other exercises, as well as which maxi-pads to wear when attending high-risk events such as Chonda Pierce concerts.

It was amazing what we all had in common.

And don't even get me started on what babies and birthdays do to our breasts.

I've always wanted to take up jogging, but my time has passed. I might have gotten away with it in my twenties, but these days I'd not only come home with shin splints but black eyes as well.

When I was a teenager the burning question in my mind was, Who am I and what is my significance in this world?

In my twenties I wondered, How can I have an impact in my career, community, and family?

I don't know how I get myself into these kinds of conversations with women I've known all of seven minutes, but this is not an unusual experience for me.

In my thirties I asked, How can I leave this world a better place for my children?

Now that I'm forty what I *really* want to know is, Where do my breasts go when I lay down?

Remember that song we learned as kids? The words went, "Do your ears hang low, do they wobble to and fro? Can you tie them in a knot? Can you tie them in a bow?" When I was eleven I thought it was hilarious to sing about feminine body parts other than ears. I had no idea one day it would come true.

The Bible says there's nothing new under the sun. This is one of the reasons I know other women deal with the same questions and issues that I do. The other reason I know this is because they tell me.

Women talk to each other about these things. I don't know if men dig deep into their souls for these kinds of intimate confessions when they get together, but I have my doubts. My friend Beth says sometimes she eavesdrops on her teenage son when he's on the phone with his friends. She says teenage boys can be on the phone for hours and exchange less than nine words in the process.

I asked, "So what are they doing?"

She tilted her head, trying to remember. "Oh, I don't know. Burping mostly."

Which, now that I think about it, seems a far more intimate exchange than the mere telling of bladder stories.

Maybe they're onto something after all.

A Million Miles from Home

There's something else many of us women have in common, something we tend to do that men don't seem as inclined to do.

We spend an awful lot of time in our heads. Really, we do. Our bodies are one place, but our heads are a million miles away fretting about the past, worrying about the future, or dissecting some problem.

I've been trying to keep track of how often I do this, how often my body and my thoughts are miles apart. It happens to me all the time. For example, when I'm working in my office, I'm thinking I should be spending more time with my kids. While playing with my kids, I'm thinking about the phone calls I should be making. Driving carpool, when I could be asking my girls about their day at school, I'm mentally perfecting the parting shot I wish I'd delivered during a recent marital spat. In church, instead of being present for worship, I'm wincing over the painful memory of my latest Visa bill and reorganizing my finances in my head. While making love to my husband, I'm wondering if anyone will get salmonella from eating the chicken I defrosted on the kitchen counter overnight.

Not to mention the hours I spend THINKING about living instead of actually DOING it.

I've spent hours redecorating my house. In my head. I could have painted the Sistine Chapel in the time I spent just *thinking* about taking my living room walls from green to beige. And if I spent half as much time dieting and exercising as I do *planning* to diet and exercise, I'd be a fashion model by now. Not to mention all the times I realize I've just spent several hours *thinking* about praying about some burden without once ever actually broaching the subject in prayer.

I don't know about you, but I also tend to wander in the land of "what ifs." I can really get lost thinking about my "what if" life complete with a size nine body, the perfect marriage, foolproof finances, and effortless romance. And I'm in good company. If I weren't, the entire romance novel industry would be waiting tables or on food stamps. Other examples of recreational escapism that leave reality in the dust? On-line chatting comes to mind, as does spending hours hypnotized by the boob tube.

I'm all for a little rejuvenating getaway now and then. But escapism can become a habit that robs us of life in the here and now.

Living in the Present

How can we bring our heads back home and get more out of life in the process?

Here's what I'm trying. See if it works for you.

"That Tree Is Green"

A little over a year ago I started seeing a wonderful Christian counselor by the name of John. I remember that in one of our first sessions together, he interrupted whatever it was we were talking about, leaned forward, and said simply, "You're not here. Be here. Present. With me. In this room."

I said, "'Scuse me?"

He said, "You're reciting events and feelings from the past. Things that happened yesterday, last week, last month. What about right now? Tell me what you're seeing, hearing, feeling this very minute."

It seemed like a perfectly reasonable request.

That is, until I couldn't do it.

I'm not kidding. I couldn't do it. I drew a blank. Completely.

That's when I knew my mind/body chasm was approaching Grand Canyon proportions.

That week, I watched myself closely. I realized I was spending a lot of my life distracted and "traveling." I also realized that, in the process, I was spending a lot of perfectly safe hours—hours when I was warm, comfy, and loved, when no crisis was looming and no one was hassling me—"borrowing" pain from yesterday or worry from tomorrow.

I vowed to make a change.

Several afternoons later, I was driving to our church with Kaitlyn beside me in the passenger seat and Kacie in the back. Suddenly I said, "That tree is green."

> "I'm being here. Here and nowhere else. I'm practicing being *present.*"

Kaitlyn said, "What?"

I said, "And the sky is blue. There are a few clouds, but not many, and the sun feels warm coming through the window. I'm driving. I'm driving my car, and Kacie is wiggling in her seat belt behind me, and Kaitlyn is sitting beside me looking at me like I'm a candidate for a straitjacket."

Kaitlyn started laughing. "What ARE you doing?"

I looked at her. "I'm being here. Here and nowhere else. With you and Kacie, in this car, right now. I'm practicing being *present.* That's what I'm doing."

I still practice. Practice emptying my head of past hurts and future concerns and any current problem that isn't tangible and present at that very moment. I concentrate on my senses, what I can see, touch, hear, taste, and smell, then and there. And sometimes, as I'm seeing, touching, hearing, tasting, and breathing, I say a simple prayer: "Thanks God, for the here and now."

Banning Carrots

So I'm learning to be "present" in my life by concentrating on the here and now and, in the process, taking a mini-vacation from yesterday's wounds or tomorrow's worries. My guess is that you might benefit from the same thing.

There's something else you and I can do that will help us experience greater joy in our lives—*today*—and it has to do with reconsidering our penchant for running pell-mell after fleet-footed rooty vegetables.

I'm talking, of course, about chasing dangling carrots.

Am I the only woman who does that? Chases the unattainable? Pursues the nonexistent? Hungers for pie in the sky when the bird in the hand would make a tasty supper all by itself?

Am I the only woman who hungers for pie in the sky when the bird in the hand would make a tasty supper all by itself?

Nah. No doubt you've run the same futile race.

So what carrots do you chase?

I'll tell you what gets me trotting. The embarrassing truth is that I'm in love with my junk mail. I am particularly enamored with mail-order catalogs. I never throw a single catalog away. Once it arrives at my home, a catalog has found a home for life. I have catalogs that have been members of my family longer than my children. I have catalogs that have been around so long they have started receiving their *own* junk mail. Several are even eligible for Social Security.

I enjoy satisfying, long-term relationships with my junk mail because I am absolutely, unequivocally, indisputably certain beyond a shadow of a doubt that somewhere in the pages of these magic wish-books exists the houseware, dress, appliance, shoe tree, nose hair trimmer, cellulite zapper, bug vacuum, push-up bra, fluorescent CD rack, buckwheat pillow,

84

facial pore steamer, glow-in-the-dark watch, or diet aid that will revolutionize my life.

It's got to be in there, I just know it. The single product that will make me organized and beautiful and whole.

So that's one of the carrots I chase.

Another one of my favorite carrots comes in the shape of home plan magazines. Magazines filled with floor plans of English Tudors, Southern mansions, New England cottages, California ranches, Craftsman bungalows. The last time I checked, my stack of magazines was taller than my German shepherd. At four bucks a pop, I have enough money invested in home plan magazines to buy a Winnebago.

> **The embarrassing truth is that I'm in love with my junk mail.**

I say that my collection of home plan magazines is another way of chasing carrots because I have this niggling feeling that, somewhere in the pages of floor plans, there exists "The Perfect House." Once I find it, I have only to build it and move in and my life will be perfect. Suddenly my relationships and possessions will cease to misbehave. My home will always smell like fresh baked bread. My days of missing deadlines will be long gone. Old-fashioned roses will bloom merrily against a white picket fence. In my perfect house—with the perfect floor plan—entertaining will be a snap. Next to me, Martha Stewart will exhibit the homemaking skills of Peg Bundy.

I realize that I am not the only woman who chases carrots, who fantasizes that with the right gadget, dress, or floor plan, her life would be perfect. I know women who chase the Perfect Man. Or the Perfect Body. Or the Perfect Hair Color. Or the Perfect Balance in their checkbook. I know women whose carrots are carats.

Just today I bought a tube of lipstick. As I stood at the cosmetics counter at Dillards shelling out seventeen bucks, my

Don't Worry, Be Happy . . .

My friend Belinda Bai quotes a Chinese proverb: "Don't borrow sorrow from tomorrow." I think of that phrase often, particularly when I'm trying to embrace the here and now. Along the same line of thought, Jane Johnson Struck addressed the concept of "fasting from worry" in her article "Time for a Change" (January/February 1988 issue of *Today's Christian Woman*). Here's an excerpt of what she had to say:

"When my husband had to undergo biopsies for cancer, I was anxious. But once he completed radiation treatments and life went on, I *really* fell into the worry trap. . . . I remembered some advice I'd given my daughter Sarah when she was in grade school [and] would lie awake at night worrying about our house catching on fire. 'Sarah,' I'd tell her, 'pretend your mind's a television set, and you're switching the channel. Now watch something happy, like family vacation memories!'

"Years later, it was time to taste my own medicine. . . . Each time I found worries swallowing up my thought life, I forced myself to *change the channel*. I'd intentionally focus on something concrete and pleasant—cardinals perched on the feeder, the winter sunset tinting the sky a frigid crimson—to blot out my preoccupation with 'what ifs.' Or I'd repeat a favorite Scripture such as Psalm 94:19 (TLB): 'Lord, when doubts fill my mind, when my heart is in turmoil, quiet me and give me renewed hope and cheer.' I determinedly tried to 'take captive' every negative thought 'to make it obedient to Christ' (2 Cor. 10:5 NIV).

"If someone told me to just stop worrying, I'd say impossible. But I decided to try it for a week—with the help of God's Spirit and his Word. While I didn't become perfectly peaceful, for those seven days I felt healthier and more optimistic than I had for quite a while."

fifteen-year-old daughter looked over at my sister and said, "That's a lot of money for a tube of lipstick."

Michelle patted Kaitlyn's arm and said, "When you get older, you'll understand. The right shade of lipstick can change your whole life."

See? My sentiments exactly.

The Art of Contentment

I don't know about you, but I'd sure like a bigger dose of joy and sanity in my life. And if you feel the same way, here's a thought: What would happen if you and I stopped chasing past hurts, future worries, and pie-in-the-sky promises of perfection in our lives? What benefits might we reap if we got in the habit of showing up in our own lives and enjoying what we have and who we are in the here and now?

Don't get me wrong. I'm not saying there aren't seasons in our lives when we need to grieve, plan, or strive, because there are. But when these become our daily default mode rather than a chosen response, my guess is that you and I miss out on a lot of joy in our lives.

Maybe it comes down to practicing contentment. I know this is an old-fashioned word that seems to have gone the way of the wooly mammoth and the rotary dial phone, but perhaps it deserves to be resurrected.

And even if you and I can't be content with *everything* going on in our lives, certainly each day we should be able to find much we can look at and smile and say, "This is good. This is enough."

A few months ago my family was sitting around the dining room table at my folks' house celebrating my dad's birthday. Over cake and ice cream, my dad looked over at my grandma and teased, "Mamaw, bet you never thought the little boy you raised would grow up to be so mean and ugly."

Without blinking an eye, Mamaw said, "What you is, is what I love."

To this day Mamaw's words—spoken with equal parts love and mischief—make me smile.

They inspire me too.

Can I love my life? Just as it is? Even when it feels a country mile shy of perfect? Can I stop escaping into my woes, worries, or fantasies and learn to be present in my life today, embracing whatever it holds—the good, the bad, and the ugly too? I'll try if you will.

Ready? So here's our plan: Show up in our lives. Enjoy it when we get there.

Even if jogging *does* give us black eyes.

8

....

Go Tubeless

Last night the girls and I were cruising the Castle Rock outlet mall with my sister Michelle when I overheard Kaitlyn complain to her aunt, "My mom won't let me wear tube tops."

Michelle said, "Your mother has a scary history with tube tops. That's probably why she won't let you get near them."

Kaitlyn said, "Really?"

Michelle nodded knowingly. "Yes. Very traumatic."

It was my turn to say, "Oh *really?*"

Ignoring me, Michelle leaned in closer to Kaitlyn and said, "She used to wear them when she was a teenager. But she had this terrible problem of always popping out of them at the most inopportune times. One time it was in front of the big picture window in our living room. She was just walking by, minding her own business when—*boiiing!* That was just one incident, yes, but there were others. This is why she is raising you tube-free. It stems from her own childhood issues."

I started laughing. I'd forgotten about the incident in the living room. And even though Michelle had her tongue firmly planted in her cheek, her memory was better than mine. There

HAD been other times when that flimsy piece of apparel had failed me miserably.

Perhaps those embarrassing teenhood moments have, indeed, shaped my current fashion policies. Now that I think about it, they've probably shaped more than that.

The truth is, I have an aversion to all sorts of tubes.

Take, for example, my relationship with toothpaste tubes. It's dysfunctional at best, downright hostile at worst. I say this because I've yet to own a tube of Crest that doesn't end up christening every other personal hygiene item in my bathroom drawer with smears and globs of sticky toothpaste.

> I've yet to own a tube of Crest that doesn't end up christening every other personal hygiene item in my bathroom drawer with smears and globs of sticky toothpaste.

Tube socks? As far as I'm concerned, they're nothing but mittens for feet and should be banned right along with any '80s surfer-type who still says "Tubular, man" when stoked.

And those drive-through banking tubes? If you ask me, they're treacherous. They lure you into the drive-through lane with the promise of convenience, but no matter where you park they're always located exactly three inches beyond your outstretched fingers, not to mention the fact that drive-through tellers have been specially trained to write your balance down on your deposit receipt only when your balance is positive. If you're overdrawn they are supposed to push a secret button that opens the speaker not only to your car but to every other car sitting in every other drive-through lane in America, including those of Dairy Queen and even some dry cleaners, before addressing you by name and telling you that you have no balance and they're returning your checks so fast they had to bring John McEnroe out of retirement to handle the job.

There's another wayward tube in my life. It's in your life too, and if you and I want to bring a little sanity back into our stressed-out lives, it might not hurt for us to reevaluate our relationship with this particular item.

I'm talking, of course, about the boob tube.

TV or Not TV

For years I've dreamed of living in a TV-free home. It's not that I don't enjoy TV (I was, in fact, addicted to *thirtysomething* and needed therapy when Gary died in a car accident on the same evening everyone was celebrating Nancy's cancer victory). Indeed, I can get as lost in that flickering blue glow as the next person.

Which is why I sometimes fantasize about throwing out the tube and seeing what life would be like without its pervasive touch.

In fact, it's been weeks since we moved to Colorado, and I have yet to call the satellite company and order service. Everybody has some sort of satellite or cable service around here, because regular TV reception in our foothills neighborhood is pretty poor. We've been watching videos and a few staticky news reports, but other than that our viewing has been severely curtailed.

I love it.

Every day Larry asks me if I've called the satellite company. And every day I tell him I haven't gotten around to it yet. He has no idea that, if I have my druthers, it'll be spring of 2010 before I find the time to make the call.

My family doesn't exactly share my passion for tubeless living.

But I still have hope. I have this hope because a couple years ago we actually survived an entire week without TV of any kind.

It all started when I sold *Today's Christian Woman* magazine on the idea of my family going "media unplugged" for seven days so I could write an article about our experiences. Jane Struck and the editorial team loved the idea. They scheduled the article for publication and gave me a deadline.

Now all I had to do was inform my family.

It all started civilly enough. We were sitting at Burger King when I decided to break the news. I figured the "beat-around-the-bush" approach might be the best way to begin.

> It all started civilly enough. We were sitting at Burger King when I decided to break the news.

"I'm writing an article," I announced. "It's about a family that goes media 'unplugged' for an entire week."

Larry said, "Unplugged?"

"Sure. You know. They unplug themselves from high-tech entertainment for a week. That means no TV, computer games, or surfing the Net. When it comes to rest and relaxation, they have to do it the old-fashioned way, relying on 'archaic' resources like imagination, conversation, books, nature . . ."

Kaitlyn looked thoughtful. "That would be interesting," she said. "But you'll never be able to write the article."

"Why not?"

"You'll never find a family to agree to do it. They'd have to be morons. They'd have to be idiots. They'd have to be—"

"—us," I said. "The family in the article is going to be us."

"I'd LOVE to help," Kaitlyn said breezily, "but I'm spending that week at Lynzee's house."

"You don't even know what week it is."

"Whatever week you choose, I won't be here."

About that time Larry came to my aid. He said, "Kaitlyn, don't be silly. It's a great idea. We'll learn all sorts of wonderful things about each other." He patted my hand. "It's a fabulous idea, Karen. In fact, let's do it right away. Not next week, because we'll want to prepare, but after that. Yes, that'll work just fine. Let's nail it down. Week after next. I'm behind you, honey."

My eyes glistened with gratitude. "Oh, sweetheart! Thank you. I thought for sure you'd hate the idea."

"Not at all. You can count on me."

"What a shame you won't be able to join us, Dad." Kaitlyn flashed him a payback smile. "We'll be sure to tell you how it goes."

I blinked. "What are you talking about?"

"Mom, don't you get it? That's the week Dad's in Taiwan on business."

Larry looked sheepish. "Oh, yeah. Must have slipped my mind."

We picked a week when everyone would be home. To prepare for the coming media fast, we glutted ourselves on electronic stimuli, playing computer games for hours and watching reruns of all our favorite TV shows. And when we weren't sitting comatose in front of glowing screens, we were at Wal-Mart buying board games and puzzles and squirreling them away like nuts in anticipation of a winter of famine.

As I drifted to sleep the night before "The Big Experiment," I pondered the coming week. Perhaps the assignment wasn't fair. After all, every member of my family had their favorite media addiction: Kaitlyn was religious about *Seventh Heaven*. Kacie, who was three at the time, was in the habit of drawing daily nourishment from all the Disney videos she had committed to memory. Larry was addicted to a computer game called War-Craft II, often launching the game after dinner and crawling into bed at 4:00 A.M. having finally defeated all the Zorgs.

I, on the other hand, don't watch much TV. I don't play video games. I e-mail my friends, but since many of them are business associates as well—and we all agreed we could still use the computer for work and school—I figured I had a loophole. Our media fast might torment my family, but my life would remain largely unchanged.

Boy, was I in for the surprise of my life.

Good-bye Aladdin, Hello Dr. Seuss

At eight A.M. on Monday I kissed Larry and Kaitlyn good-bye, then went to wake Kacie. With a full day of writing before me, my plan was to take Kacie to the babysitter's before nine. But after a quick touch of Kacie's fevered cheek, I realized my day was taking an unexpected detour.

Unable to take her to the sitter's—or plant her in front of the TV—I soon found myself juggling Dr. Seuss, deadlines, and Dimetapp. I made Kacie a nest of blankets in my office, jumping up from behind my desk every few minutes to refill juice or read her a story or rescue Barbie from the jaws of Walter. How I longed to pop in a video for a ninety-minute break!

Midafternoon Kacie fell asleep. I was thrilled that I could *finally* get some work done, although I wondered if I'd get the Bad Mother of the Year Award for feeling grateful for a fever-induced nap.

> I wondered if I'd get the Bad Mother of the Year Award for feeling grateful for a fever-induced nap.

As I hustled to get a few necessities done, an uncomfortable realization dogged my thoughts. I wasn't addicted to the television. But I was more than happy to benefit from the addiction of my children. How many hours each day had I been encouraging Kacie to zone out with Ariel and Aladdin and Anastasia so I could complete some menial task without interruption? It was a sobering thought!

Open for Negotiation

At dinnertime, my family regrouped for the evening. They also tried to reopen negotiations.

Kaitlyn raised an eyebrow as I pulled a steaming bowl of vegetables from the microwave. "I think if I have to miss *Seventh Heaven* tonight, you shouldn't get to use the microwave."

"Cooking isn't entertainment. We're only nixing high-tech entertainment."

"I think watching you cook is pretty entertaining, especially when you set things on fire. Are you sure it doesn't count?"

"I'll ban the microwave if you'll eat cold food," I conceded. "Never mind."

Next, it was Larry's turn. "Isn't the goal to spend more time together as a family?" he said. "I think if we all agree to do something—like watch a video or play a computer game—as long as we're doing it together, it should be allowed."

I smiled. "Nice try."

The wheedling eventually stopped. And that's when things started to get interesting.

First, dinner began differently. Dinner normally requires an eleven-minute preamble as I repeat the following five phrases, averaging three repetitions per phrase, in random order: "Dinner's on the table." "Turn off the TV right now and come eat." "Didn't you hear me?" "No, you can't finish the show." "I SAID TURN OFF THE TV AND COME EAT!"

This time I asked once.

They came.

Best yet, they stayed.

Normally, my family wolfs and runs. I think the unspoken goal is to be out of the kitchen before the last bite of food hits the lining of the stomach. This is because many children (and even a few husbands) have this phobia that, if they are ever caught loitering in a kitchen, something terrible will happen to them. For example, they might be asked to carry a glass from the table to the sink. This, of course, is far worse than being asked to make a bed, but not nearly as traumatic as cleaning a bathroom.

The other reason family members tend to eat and run is because they hear their names being called by the Internet, video games, and TV shows. But on the first night of our little media fast, these voices were silenced. And lo and behold, my husband and children actually lingered around the dinner table.

Even Walter got in on the act. Before long, Larry had invented some sort of game where he was sliding our gangly dog repeatedly across the linoleum floor, which for some reason our daughters found hysterically funny. The laughter was still bouncing off the kitchen walls as I dried the last dish and put it away.

I had hoped the media ban would get rid of some of the noise in my home. Boy, was I wrong! The house was noisier than ever. And the sounds were like music to my ears.

Getting the Shakes

Larry understood the rules. Kaitlyn understood the rules. Kacie was in a league all her own.

By day three, Kacie needed a cartoon, and she needed it bad.

Sitting with her at the kitchen table, I tried one more time to explain why we were doing what we were doing.

By day three, Kacie needed a cartoon, and she needed it bad.

"You see, Kacie, there's this magazine, and I told them I would write an article—"

I could see this was flying like a lead balloon. Trying a different approach, I said: "Kacie, remember last night when you and Dad had that wrestling match? Well, what would you rather do? Have an exciting wrestling match with your dad, or watch some boring old cartoon that you've seen a hundred times?"

"Watch TV."

"And what about this morning? Think of all the puzzles we did. Wasn't that fun? Would you rather play with me or watch TV?"

"Watch TV."

The kid was scaring me.

Actually, what was scaring me was seeing how deeply the television had infiltrated and impacted our lives.

Well, if I couldn't get her to see the logic of what we were doing, I'd have to secure her cooperation by other means.

That evening Larry appeared in the doorway of the den where I sat reading a book. "I just heard an interesting rumor," he grinned.

"Really? What was it?"

"Something about the TV."

"The TV?"

"Something you told Kacie."

I squirmed. "Kacie?"

"She told me why she can't watch cartoons anymore. She said you told her the TV is *broken*."

"I never actually *said* the word *broken*. My *exact* words were, 'Look, Kacie, there's no picture!' And there's not. There's just static. I tuned the TV to channel zero."

Larry wagged a finger. "If you're going to tattle on us for this assignment, you have to tell the WHOLE story. I expect to read about this in your article."

"Fine," I muttered. I supposed it was only fair. Besides, I hear confession is good for the soul.

It's About Time

In the following days, I was amazed how much more time we had, individually and as a family.

How did we fill that time? Games and puzzles came in handy. One of our favorites was Hot Potato, where we tossed a musical stuffed-toy potato around the room. Whoever was holding the potato when it burped was out of the game. (The fact that we found this so entertaining is either a testament to our creative abilities or proof that we need to get out of the house more often!)

But most rewarding was watching my girls interact in creative play. They schemed. They brainstormed. They dreamed. They ransacked my office for scissors and cardboard and markers and tape. They debated and reconciled, negotiated, bartered, and giggled.

I also noticed that it was much easier to wrangle cooperation when I wasn't competing with the Disney Channel or the World Wide Web. I can't say that Kaitlyn suddenly begged to set the table or that Kacie couldn't wait to pick up her toys, but there was definitely a marked difference in attitude. Best yet, I went a whole week without having to contend with the words, "But I can't! I'm right in the middle of a show!"

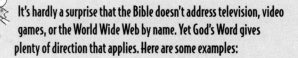

King Solomon on Chat Rooms, The Jerry Springer Show, and Howard Stern (sort of)

It's hardly a surprise that the Bible doesn't address television, video games, or the World Wide Web by name. Yet God's Word gives plenty of direction that applies. Here are some examples:

Garbage In, Garbage Out

My friend Cherie has an index card taped to the front of her TV cabinet. It reads: "I will set no worthless thing before my eyes" (Ps. 101:3). Another good verse is Philippians 4:8: "Whatever is true, whatever is honorable, whatever is right, whatever is pure, whatever is lovely, whatever is of good repute ... let your mind dwell on these things." Try using either of these verses as a benchmark as you tune in to your favorite shows this week (but take two Advil first; it may be a painful experience!).

Thanks for Sharing

You can't convince me that King Solomon wasn't writing prophetically about chat rooms, Howard Stern, and guests on the Jerry Springer Show when he penned: "A fool does not delight in understanding, but only in revealing his own mind" (Prov. 18:2).

continued on page 99

We seemed more in sync with each other as well. Perhaps it's easier to pick up on the moods of the people you live with—and then adjust your own attitude to harmonize with the group—when you're not being influenced by an influx of media adrenaline. After all, attitudes on TV are bigger-than-life: Characters are often independent or smart-alecky to a fault. When my kids watch a lot of TV, is it easier for them to align their attitudes with those of their TV friends than those of their own family members? Do Larry and I do the same?

Return to Lunacy

As the week drew to a close, everyone chattered happily about being reunited with their favorite media addiction. Larry

Birds of a Feather...

Think about most of the characters on TV. Do the words *wise* and *godly* come to mind? I didn't think so. And yet, if we were brave enough to do the math, we might have to admit we spend more quality hours with TV buddies than we do with our own family members or Christian friends. Solomon warns: "He who walks with wise men will be wise, but the companion of fools will suffer harm" (Prov. 13:20).

Relaxation or Worship?

I've always loved the phrase "practicing the presence of the Lord." After all, isn't that what praise and worship are all about? Basking in the presence of the One I love? But if that's the case, I might be in trouble, because in any given week I spend more time basking in the glow of a computer or TV screen than I do basking in the presence of the Lord. We're reminded in Matthew 6:21 that "Where your treasure is, there will your heart be also." (And in our fast-paced society, time certainly qualifies as treasure!) Is my TV or web-surfing addiction stealing just my hours, or is it impacting my heart and soul as well?

The Bible tells us not to become worshipers of images. I always figured I was safe as long as there wasn't a golden calf in my living room. Now I'm not so sure!

was anxious to reclaim Planet Earth from alien forces, Kaitlyn missed sending electronic greeting cards to her friends, and Kacie was simply relieved that the TV was going to mysteriously start working again at midnight on Sunday.

At 10:45 Sunday night, Larry and I found ourselves sitting on the living room couch and talking about the recent events. We agreed it had been an eventful week. In the past, we had tried to create quality family time by adding events to our already busy schedule, things like family game night or a Saturday event or project. Now we suspected that the best way to forge closer family bonds wasn't to program more things *into* our lives but to take a few things out.

"I'm not ready to toss out the TV and computer for good, but I wouldn't mind doing this again," I admitted. "In fact, maybe we should do this every couple months. Just to realign our perspectives. Reconfirm our priorities."

"I could go for that," Larry agreed. "But couldn't we realign and reconfirm in a weekend? Just go unplugged for a couple days instead of a week? Not Super Bowl weekend or anything like that though."

"I don't know. We'll have to negotiate on that one."

"Speaking of negotiating . . ." Larry looked at his watch. "It's almost midnight."

I grabbed his wrist and looked. It was one minute to eleven. "Yeah. Right. If you live in New York, you mean."

"Midnight in New York! That's good enough for me!" And he sprang for his laptop. So what if we began the experiment on Central Time and ended on Eastern? It had been a good week "unplugged."

Can we do it again? Do we dare? When life is feeling crazy and the members of my family are going a million different directions and feeling disconnected and frazzled, can turning off the TV help us to regroup, refocus, and reconnect, personally and corporately as well? Can turning off the TV in YOUR home help you to do the same?

I guess that's my challenge to you. Wanna improve your life? Turn off the tube.

I'd write more on this topic, but I need to go. Larry's due home any minute, and I've got to think up an excuse for not calling the satellite company today.

I've got an idea. I could always say I went to the bank to make a deposit and spent the entire day in the drive-through lane. Seems I could never quite reach that blasted tube.

9

....

Redecorate a Room
for Less than a Hundred Bucks

oes your life ever feel out of control?

Mine sure does.

Take the holidays, for example. My husband, daughters, dogs, and I spent Thanksgiving with my folks. While there, I borrowed one of my dad's computers so I could work on this book. In the process, I somehow clicked on the wrong link and managed to get his whole computer system off the network.

The next morning I didn't load my mom's coffeepot securely in the coffeemaker and, as a result, flooded her kitchen counter with freshly brewed java.

A few hours later, electric knife in hand, I was carving a ham when suddenly something popped and flashed. The kitchen lights dimmed for a heartbeat, and the smell of smoke filled the air. Turns out I'd sliced through the cord to the electric knife.

And we were still invited back for Christmas. Go figure.

I'd love a calm, uneventful life. This does not, however, appear to be my destiny.

Consider, for example, the whole belly dancing thing.

A couple years ago while living in Dallas I took belly dancing lessons. Recently, after moving to Colorado, I decided it was time to dust off my finger cymbals and find an instructor in Denver. I even talked Kaitlyn into attending the first lesson with me.

On the night we climbed into my 4Runner and headed downtown, I envisioned a quiet, run-of-the-mill evening filled with uneventful mother/daughter bonding while belly dancing. You know, slice-of-life stuff.

"Bring a hundred and forty dollars cash, unmarked bills, or you'll never see your truck again."

Kaitlyn and I followed our map to a seedy part of the city, parked the car, and hurried into the building. An hour later, we emerged from the studio. We walked across the parking lot arm in arm, laughing at ourselves, feeling very hip and bonded and relaxed.

Until we couldn't find the car.

What we found instead was a sign that said, "Private Property. Trespassers will be towed. 555-0271."

I fished my cell phone from the bottom of my purse and dialed the number. A woman answered the phone.

I said, "You don't happen to have my 4Runner, do you? Hunter green . . . Texas plates . . ."

She said, "We have it. Come to the towing yard tonight at 10:30. Bring your driver's license, car registration, and a hundred and forty dollars cash, unmarked bills, or you'll never see your truck again."

I called Larry. He and Kacie arrived an hour later in Larry's blue Beetle. We found an ATM, then followed my scribbled directions. Soon we were in the land of topless bars and pawn shops. We passed streetlamps with shot-out bulbs and the graffitied offices of bail bondsmen. At the end of a dark gravel road, the little blue bug crunched to a stop in front of the chain link fence of the towing yard. A trailer marked "Office" sat with darkened windows inside the fence.

I clutched the cash and said, "They're not here."

Suddenly a young man with dirty blond hair materialized out of the darkness. He spat once and approached the Beetle.

Larry rolled down the window.

My window.

He leaned across me and said, "We have what you asked for. Where's the car?"

The man shrugged. "Boss ain't here. You'll have to wait."

Larry said, "That wasn't the deal. You said come with the money and we've got it. We want the car and we want it now."

The man sneered. "You gotta wait for the Boss."

Larry said, "Look, you, I'm a university vice president, and you don't want to mess with me or things are going to get ugly."

No doubt somewhere in his very core—in a place far beyond what we could see with the naked eye—this man was quaking.

He laughed (a very good cover-up, I thought) and walked away.

We sat in the car a while longer, probably so Larry could choose the manner in which he was going to make things get ugly.

Meanwhile, the man sauntered back into the yard and locked the chain link gates behind him. Then he climbed into a tow truck, revved the engine, and drove the truck forward, nosing it right to the gate. He left it there, engine idling, high beams trained on our little VW, for several minutes. Then he popped the transmission into reverse and backed the truck up until it was sitting directly in front of my SUV.

I said hopefully, "Maybe he's going to bring it out to us."

Larry beamed. "He thinks we're going to storm the gate."

I think it's more likely he had simply forgotten to take his medication. He spent the next fifteen minutes moving his truck threateningly around the locked yard, keeping his high beams on us the entire time.

105

About that time the Boss arrived. We paid the ransom, reclaimed my car, and went home.

All in all, a happy ending to a chaotic evening.

Although I'm still wondering what Larry had up his sleeve. How exactly did he intend to rescue our car? What lethal weaponry had he been poised to unleash? He won't tell me what his plans were, but I have my suspicions.

I'm wondering if they had anything to do with me and an electric knife.

Calm Harbor in the Storm

No wonder I sometimes feel as though I'm going crazy. And when I'm not demolishing my parents' home or rescuing my kidnapped car, I'm chasing my two dogs or carpooling my two kids or trying to explain to my editor why my manuscript arrived in the mail sporting paw prints and smelling faintly like a German shepherd (it's a long story; don't ask).

I know your life feels crazy too.

Since this book is about celebrating life and embracing wholeness even when everything feels crazy, let me tell you about a quick fix that helps me gain the upper hand on my sometimes ungainly life.

> I move a bookshelf or paint a wall or install a new light, and suddenly I'm in charge of my life again.

I make a quick improvement in my environment.

That's it. That's all it is. I redecorate.

I move a bookshelf or paint a wall or install a new light, and suddenly I'm in charge of my life again.

I guess it shouldn't surprise anyone that there is a link between surroundings and emotions. When you walk into a room, the color of the walls, the height of a ceiling, the quantity of sunshine, the level of clutter, all make an emotional impact.

Even the way furniture is arranged. To this day, I can walk into someone's house, and if a picture is hung too high on the wall—just sort of floating above everything else in the room—I feel a vague sense of uneasiness. I don't know why. Perhaps I was attacked by a mishung portrait as a child. Whatever the reason, it's true.

And my guess is that you're the same way. Maybe not about paintings. But about something, because environment really does impact emotions. And no matter what's going on in your life right now, there's a good chance that by making even a subtle change in your environment, your spirits may be lifted as well.

> If a picture is hung too high on the wall, I feel a vague sense of uneasiness. Perhaps I was attacked by a mishung portrait as a child.

Inexpensive Room Improvements

I am not made of money, much to the dismay and chagrin of my children. And so when I feel the urge to pick up my spirits by perking up my house, I try to make improvements that don't cost an arm and a leg. Perhaps you're interested in the same kind of inexpensive pick-me-ups for your house.

If so, here are some ideas.

De-clutter

Most days, my idea of cleaning house is to sweep the room with a glance. So you can see that I'm not exactly Heloise. But even *I* have to admit that spiffing up the house or even just a room is an immediate blues-buster. And it's certainly cheap. It doesn't cost a thing to pick up the magazines and toss the clothing in the hamper and run the vacuum. In fact, stash some of that clutter in the garage for your next yard sale, and you might even *make* money in the process!

Lighting

It's amazing how even a slight change in lighting can impact the mood of an entire room. A new lamp placed in a previously unlit corner can change pretty much everything. My personal favorite lighting trick? I take a decorative tree—either real or artificial—and cover it with white Christmas lights. And not just at Christmastime. I even plug in lamp timers so my trees light up automatically at twilight. All year long. Makes me think of fireflies. Really warms up a room. In fact, back in Texas, I had a lighted tree in nearly every room in the house. Except the bathrooms. After all, who wants to feel like they're doing their business in a park?

> Most days, my idea of cleaning house is to sweep the room with a glance.

Painting

Painting is cheap. Time-consuming but cheap. And if you don't want to paint the entire room, try just one wall. Pick a wall that is already a focal point in your room—perhaps it is the backdrop for the fireplace or TV cabinet—and paint it a darker or different color. From now on, I'm going to try to select a color that is not too far off from the color of my hair. Last week I got my hair cut. Scissors in hand, the stylist said, "You must have spent the weekend painting." I said, "You're absolutely right." I decided not to mention that the weekend I spent painting occurred over two months ago.

Think Group

Rearrange your stuff so that everything exists in some sort of group. When you look around your room, you should see "blocks" of belongings. For example, that easy chair is in the same "group" as the couch and loveseat—not halfway across the room but close enough to form an intimate collection of seating. A wall clock by itself will appear to be "floating"— but put an occasional table, plant, or umbrella holder on the floor beneath it, and you've got another group. And don't hang that painting three feet above the piano—hang it low enough so that the painting, piano, and even the ficus tree next to the piano appear to be enjoying a friendly conversation together. Same with picture frames. Arrange them only an inch or two apart in groups. This works if you're arranging them on a coffee table or in a hallway gallery.

Less Is More

I just recarpeted my den. To do so, I had to empty the room of everything. Once the new carpet was laid, I took my time replenishing the room. Doodads and geegaws and trinkets

Cheap Thrills

Want to energize a tired room without dropping a wad of cash? Here are five things you can do:

1. Get rid of the clutter—be ruthless!
2. Light your room in a different way by purchasing a new lamp or moving old ones.
3. Paint a single wall or entire room and get lots of impact for a little bit of cash.
4. Arrange furniture, lamps, paintings and even greenery near each other in cozy groups rather than spread out and isolated. Remember, even the Lone Ranger had Tonto.
5. Pick one room that needs to be revitalized, then cruise the rest of your home for accessories that will complete the look you want to achieve!

and artificial greenery and baskets and piles and pillows and doilies and whatnots didn't get an automatic round-trip ticket back into the room. For some, it was a one-way trip to the garage, the Goodwill, or even to the trash. I was amazed how revitalized the room looked with half the stuff in it!

Shop Till You Drop

Want to revitalize a tired room? There's nothing like a shopping spree to help you find just the right accessories to turn a room from drab to dynamite! A new chair . . . a pillow . . . an interesting lamp . . . a painting with just the right colors . . . an artificial flower arrangement . . . a wreath or photo frame or inviting throw . . . any of these can perk up your room. Now here's the fun part: You can shop till you drop without dropping a wad of bills by *shopping in your very own home!* That's right! Easy parking and no checkout lines! Just pick the room you want to redo, then cruise the other rooms in your home for convenient treasures. Sure, it's a case of robbing Peter to pay Paul, but you'll end up with one really great-looking room and—who knows?—you might be surprised at how good your other rooms still look once the deed is done.

Giving your environment a face-lift won't change your whole life. But it feels great nevertheless. And if none of the ideas in this chapter works for you, consider a nice piece of modern art for your home. In fact, maybe I could be of service. I'm taking up ice sculpturing, and I'd be happy to whip something up for you.

That is, as soon as the new cord arrives for the electric knife.

10

....

Lose Your "Religion" . . .

My sister Michelle was sitting calmly in church one Sunday morning when she felt a little tickle in her throat. You know the drill. Tickle. Clear your throat. Cough a little. Maybe pop a lemon drop or two. Simple, right? Michelle cleared her throat.

The tickle stayed.

She gave a discreet little cough.

The tickle merely thumbed its nose at her.

She cleared her throat again, louder this time.

By now the tickle had picked up the phone and called some friends and was throwing a full-blown party in Michelle's esophagus.

Michelle stood and began excusing herself past the knees of all the folks sitting between her and the aisle. She made a beeline for the foyer, then the front door. Once outside, she let loose with a volley of violent coughs as she attempted to dislodge the tickle from its hiding place. After several minutes of can't-catch-your-breath-doubled-over-on-the-sidewalk sort of coughing, she was able to return to the sanctuary.

Unfortunately, all that coughing jarred something in her vertebrae, and several mornings later, she woke up with her back frozen in pain. She inched her way out of bed, hobbled to the closet for the cane her husband had once used with a broken foot, then phoned her chiropractor to say she was on her way.

Before long, Michelle's husband, Russ, was easing her into the front seat of his SUV with the same kind of caution and finesse a SWAT member might use while disarming a bomb. Once Michelle was settled, Russ reached for the lever to GENTLY recline her seat a few inches.

> Russ eased Michelle into the front seat of his SUV with the same kind of caution and finesse a SWAT member might use while disarming a bomb.

Suddenly WHOPPP! Michelle's seat—and Michelle—flopped all the way backwards and banged into the backseat. Michelle wailed. Russ winced. He inched her upright again, then hurried to the driver's side and revved the engine. Russ and Michelle each breathed a sigh of relief. Soon they would be at the doctor's office. Everything would be all right.

A few moments later Russ pulled up to a stoplight, and the driver next to them began honking and pointing.

Michelle stared and said, "What?"

The other driver gestured wildly.

Michelle squinted. "WHAT?"

The driver mouthed the words, "Your purse is on the roof of your car!"

The light turned green. Russ pulled sharply to the side of the road to retrieve the purse. Jumping out of the car, he slammed the door behind him, ran to Michelle's side of the car, and grabbed her purse off the roof. He couldn't believe what a fiasco this was turning out to be! What else could possibly go wrong?

Russ ran back to his side of the car. He tried the door handle. It wouldn't budge. He tried it again. The car door was locked. He gestured wildly at Michelle to open the door, but she could only look at him helplessly through the glass.

Apparently, in all the commotion, Michelle's elbow had pushed down the button that locked all the car doors. Now, her back frozen stiff, she couldn't twist enough in her seat to unlock the doors.

Russ was going to be standing there a very long time.

In fact, the only reason he's not standing there even as we speak is because Michelle remembered the cane. She couldn't twist her body enough to pull up the lock button at her shoulder, but she could use the cane to reach across the seat and hook the handle and open Russ's door for him. It took longer than you might think, however, because by then Michelle was laughing so hard it was near impossible to hold the cane steady.

You'll be glad to know that twenty-seven chiropractic sessions and several hundred dollars later, Michelle's back has recovered nicely. She's walking again, and bending and sitting comfortably. She's even going to church again. In fact, maybe you've seen her. She's the woman singing hymns while cradling a Sam's Club–sized bag of lemon drops in her lap.

Molehills to Mountains

Ever have days like that? Days when something starts out simple and ends up all convoluted and complex?

My guess is that you too have experienced days or weeks when normal circumstances sort of snowball out of your control. You start the day like a perfectly sane person and by midmorning you're locked in a car, waving a cane at your husband who is standing in a busy street holding your purse, and you're laughing so hard you don't know if you're going to need CPR or a dry pair of panties.

I have days like that.

I also have days when my life gets all complicated—not because of a series of mishaps—but because I have the knack of making life harder than it needs to be.

You know the ol' molehill to mountain scenario? That happens to be the story of my life. Well, the Cliff Notes version anyway.

Like what I do with diets.

Every time I decide to renew my commitment to healthier eating and exercise, I spend hours getting ready. I make lists, design charts, organize menus, set goals. I create reward systems using cute little stickers from the stationery store. I rally a network of girlfriends to cheer me on. I buy new walking shoes, new batteries for my Walkman cassette player, and new sunglasses because, hey, I've got a sunglass fetish and any excuse will do.

I make photocopies of daily food and activity logs and organize them in three-ring binders, one sheet per day from now until the year 2007. I talk half my friends into joining me in my quest for the size nine body and then make notebooks for each of them.

The last time I started a diet, I spent $57 at Kinkos making photocopies. Unfortunately the only thing I lost was the top layer of skin on my fingertips from collating all those stupid notebooks.

I can spend months getting ready to diet without ever consuming a single carrot. I can spend hundreds of dollars preparing to exercise without ever breaking into a sweat.

Now, I'm not saying I NEVER get a diet started. Sometimes I do. But even then, I usually make it more difficult than it needs to be. Even then, sometimes I try too hard.

Like the time I was experiencing a self-control meltdown and e-mailed a friend of mine in a panic. I wrote:

"Help! I'm feeling stressed and overwhelmed and all I want to do is go to the freezer and eat a chocolate ice-cream sandwich. So far, in order to avoid eating this ice-cream sandwich, I've consumed four bananas, six bagels with lowfat cream cheese, five containers of Yoplait nonfat yogurt, nine sticks of fat-free mozzarella cheese, and now I'm writing to you in a desperate attempt to keep my hands occupied so they don't lead me to the freezer and feed me, against my will, the ice-cream sandwich that is continuing to call my name even as I type."

The next morning my friend e-mailed me back and said, "I think you should have eaten the ice-cream sandwich."

And it was good advice. If I had eaten the ice-cream sandwich and satisfied my craving, by my calculations I would have actually consumed 3,475 fewer calories than I managed to consume by NOT eating the ice-cream sandwich.

Sometimes I think I forget to K.I.S.S.—"Keep it simple, stupid."

Remember, I even managed to complicate my mammogram. I mean, what's up with that? All I had to do was make one phone call, drive four miles to the Women's Imaging Center, and stand there not screaming while some technician in a pink lab coat reduced my mammary glands to the thickness of two-ply toilet paper. Piece of cake, right? In fact, what could be more straightforward?

Instead, I managed to take something relatively simple— "Get a mammogram and get it now"—and complicate it to no end with dark thoughts and borrowed fears. As a result, it took me four months to make that one simple phone call. Lucky for me, the lump I'd felt turned out to be nothing. But by turning a molehill into a mountain, I ran the risk of turning a little lump into a challenging crisis.

> The next morning my friend e-mailed me back and said, "I think you should have eaten the ice-cream sandwich."

Sometimes we make things so much more complicated than they need to be. We try too hard to manage our emotions and our lives, and sometimes, in the process, we end up complicating everything beyond reason.

Like the whole God thing.

I'm starting to wonder if, when it comes to spiritual matters, we haven't turned molehills into mountains. I mean, we seem to have taken something fairly straightforward—a relationship—and turned it into something that is NOT straightforward, namely, religion.

I'm wondering if there's not a simpler way.

> When it comes to spiritual matters, we seem to have taken something fairly straightforward–a relationship–and turned it into something that is NOT straightforward, namely, religion. I'm wondering if there's not a simpler way.

Crash and Burn

In my book *Sometimes I Wake Up Grumpy . . . and Sometimes I Let Him Sleep* I wrote about this sort of crash-and-burn crisis that happened in my marriage and to my emotions several years ago. During that time I alternated between—how can I say this delicately?—rage, rage, and more rage as I came to grips with a number of destructive patterns my husband and I had managed to forge in our years together.

Okay, I guess there was more than just rage. Throw some depression and rebellion into the mix, and you've probably got a pretty fair picture of my life for a number of months.

My faith also crashed and burned.

It didn't happen right away. But about eighteen months into my little crisis, I felt as though the tornado that had swept through my emotions was starting to pass. Larry and I were attending counseling and trying to figure out what had gone wrong, and my rage had subsided into mere fury. I wasn't sure if the winds had passed or if I was in the eye of the storm, but

I knew I was, somehow, in considerably less turmoil than I'd been several months earlier.

That's when I took a good look at my life and realized I was no longer certain that God existed.

I don't shock myself too often, but I have to admit, I was shocked by these new thoughts. After all, I'd accepted Jesus Christ as my Savior when I was a kid, and my relationship with him has always been a foundation of my life. I married someone who shared my faith, I taught my children to love the Lord, and I've always loved going to church for the encouragement, fellowship, teaching, and—best of all—the experience of enjoying the presence of God that waits for me behind the stained glass doors.

The terrain of my very soul had been ravaged, and landmarks both familiar and immovable—including my faith in God—had been altered in the wake of the storm.

Suddenly I was questioning it all.

At the time, I was involved in a discussion group. We'd been reading and discussing Max Lucado's book *A Distant Thunder*. Ours was a small gathering consisting of several longtime friends. Oddly enough, my doubts didn't keep me home. I showed up each Wednesday night as always—I just brought my cynicism and questions with me.

One night I looked at these friends and said, "It's like I've just been through this horrible storm. The wind raged and the rain came down in droves and the earth shook. And suddenly it's over, and I open my front door and look outside, and I can't believe my eyes. I don't recognize anything! The forest that was over there is gone. The skyscraper on the horizon has been leveled. The river that ran north and south now runs east and west. There's an unfamiliar mountain to my left, and when I look to my right there's an ocean where I used to walk the dog. Nothing is the same. All the landmarks that I've used for years to get my bearings . . . they're all changed or gone. The storm changed everything in its wake, and immovable things that were once as familiar to me as the back of my own hand are gone or changed into something else entirely."

And that's exactly what it felt like. The terrain of my very soul had been ravaged, and landmarks both familiar and immovable—including my faith in God—had been altered in the wake of the storm.

What's It All about, Alfie?

Talk about going crazy! Trust me when I say that nothing will make you doubt your sanity quicker than finding yourself suddenly asking hard questions about God.

Like, Is he even really up there?

I imagine some folks go their entire lives without a major crisis of faith. I used to think I'd be one of them.

At least I'm in good company. Monk and poet Thomas Merton wrote: "With deep faith comes deep doubt." Philip Yancey wrote a book about faith crises entitled *Disappointment with God.* C. S. Lewis's faith hit the skids in the aftermath of the death of his beloved wife.

David's doubts fill the Psalms.

Peter had faith enough to walk to Jesus across the water, but when he saw the waves, the Bible says he was filled with doubt and began to sink.

And when Jesus tells a desperate father, "I can heal your son if you'll only believe," the man cries out, "Lord, I *do* believe! Help my unbelief!"

Luckily for you and for me, God's not a pixie.

In the book *Peter Pan* by J. M. Barrie, Peter tells Wendy, "Every time a child says, 'I don't believe in fairies,' there is a fairy somewhere that falls down dead."

118

I didn't believe.
But God was still on the throne.

Choosing God

Sometimes we look for miracles. Sometimes they come looking for us. And, sometimes, the reason they finally find us is because we're just too tired to get out of the way.

One night I felt so restless I just had to get out of the house even though it was past midnight. With a reckless attitude, I laced up my walking shoes and hit the pavement around my neighborhood. I walked for a long time, crying and thinking and maybe praying, if you can call it praying when someone who doesn't even believe in God anymore cries out for answers.

Tears on my face, I walked for more than an hour, sometimes stopping in the middle of the street to look up and search the stars for some sign of the God who had hung them there. I asked a hundred questions, most of which started with the word "Why . . .?" The heavens were beautiful that night, cold and clear, but silent. Still, I sobbed and walked and talked, maybe to myself, maybe to God; I couldn't say for sure.

At the end of that hour, I decided to believe that God is real. That was it. No handwriting in the sky, no thunderous voice of assurance, not a single winged messenger. Just a decision to believe. And I decided to believe in God for the simple reason that the alternative was too horrible to even consider: Without God, life was coincidental and capricious at best, hostile and hopeless at worst. I decided that believing in God—even if I were wrong—was the only option that made any sense.

Now that I believed in God again, what next? What was I going to do with him? Fight him? Ignore him? Embrace him?

I turned toward home, my legs tired and eyes swollen from the tears I'd cried. My heart still felt wounded, though drained of the angst that had driven me into the darkness. There were all sorts of new questions to ponder, but I figured they'd keep a while longer, maybe even long enough for God and me to tackle them together. All I knew was that it was nearly 2:00 in the morning, and I was a half mile from home, and, for the first time in months, the thing I needed even more than answers was a good night's sleep.

Starting from Scratch

I grew up in Southern California where earthquakes are not uncommon. Every year there are tremors. Every couple years there's a quake that lands us on the national news.

And every dozen years or so, after a particularly rambunctious quake—the kind that makes freeways roll like a seascape and brick chimneys fall into themselves—you'll see a wrecking ball taking down a building. Maybe that building had a few small structural flaws—small enough to go unnoticed for forty years, big enough so that when it was time to rock and roll, the building failed. In time, someone will build something better and stronger in its place, but for now there's merely smoke and rubble.

Sometimes you gotta start from scratch.

After all, don't doctors rebreak mismended bones so they can heal stronger? And don't farmers scorch their fields so new growth can begin?

My faith had been leveled. Only smoke and rubble remained.

Would a new faith emerge in its place? Perhaps even a stronger faith?

I had no idea, but I imagined I was about to find out.

11

··

. . . and Embrace a Relationship Instead

W hen we last left our heroine, she was weary of foot and soul. After making a simple decision to believe in God again, she continued living her life a day at a time, all the while wondering if and when God would begin to make his presence known again in her life.

Seriously, I'd love to say that my faith just sort of bounced back the moment I decided to believe in God again. But in reality, I felt like a skittish horse.

What did a relationship with a holy God really mean?

What did he expect of me anyway?

What if he asked me to stay in a wounded marriage? What if he—and I wasn't sure how I felt about this—wanted to *fix* my marriage?

My mom said, "It's not about a marriage. It's about you. What he wants is a relationship with YOU."

But I wasn't sure what that even meant anymore.

Wake-up Call

One morning my phone rang at 6:15.

I jerked my head from my drool-ridden pillow and groped for the phone. "'llo?"

"Get dressed. I'm kidnapping you. I'll be there in an hour."

It was Beth.

"Kidnapping?" I mumbled. "Sure. Okay. See you in an hour."

"Get dressed. I'm kidnapping you. I'll be there in an hour."

I pulled on some clothes, ran a brush through my hair and mascara wand through my lashes. It wasn't until I was sitting in Beth's Aztec and she was merging onto the freeway that she finally told me where we were going.

She said, "You need spiritual CPR."

I said, "Say what?"

"I'm taking you to a charismatic service. Christ for the Nations has their campus here in town, and every morning they have an hour-long praise and worship service. I know that you grew up in a charismatic church, yet you've attended Baptist churches for the past eight years—I'm wondering if your problem is that you're a Pentecostal trapped in a Baptist's body!"

I had to laugh.

I adored our little Baptist church even though it was, of course, different from the charismatic churches I'd attended and also loved. Beth, on the other hand, was Baptist through and through. Look up the word *Baptist* in the dictionary and you'll find Beth's picture. I doubted she'd ever stepped foot in a charismatic service in her life. I looked at Beth. "Think you can handle it?"

She grinned. "Nope, but what are friends for?"

We attended the service. It was vivacious and lively and beautiful and sincere. And I was amazed how closed my heart felt through it all.

I returned home and hopped in the shower, and that's when the tears began. They were tears that came from a deep place and seemed to return to that same place. I cried off and on that entire day, and I wasn't even sure why.

Baby Steps

I'd been in counseling for about six months when John and I landed on the topic of prayer.

I said, "I haven't been praying at all."

John said, "I know."

I said, "I'm afraid. I'm afraid I can't live up to the standard, that I can't make the grade. I SHOULD be able to forgive my husband for past hurts. I SHOULD be able to be a loving Christian wife. I SHOULD be able to live victoriously and happily ever after. I SHOULD be able to do all these things, but I can't. And I'm afraid if I start praying again, God will ask me to do the things I can't do. I think I'm making progress—at least I believe again that he's up there—but we're not exactly on speaking terms yet."

John said, "This is what I do. Every morning I kneel in my living room and log on-line with God, so to speak. I say, 'Okay, Lord, here I am. I'm asking you to show up in my life today, to live today through me. You be the one doing it, because on my own, I'm going to fall short. Be with me today, living the Christian walk through me, through your power and not mine, because I can't do it any other way. Amen.' Then I get up and begin my day."

I thought a moment, then said, "That sounds simple enough."

He said, "It is."

I said, "Maybe I could do that."

He said, "Yes, you could."

I said, "I think I'd like to try."

Three weeks later I had yet to pray that prayer, not one single morning. I kept forgetting. One day in John's office I said,

"Whoops, I'd better write this down, make myself a note or a list or something, to remind myself to pray."

John said, "Don't make it so complicated! A list means you're trying to force yourself to do it on your own, in your own power. Making a list is *religion,* not *relationship.* Instead, as you drive home today pray, 'Lord, remind me this week to talk to you every morning, will you? I want to do this but, left on my own, to be honest, I'm probably going to forget, just like I've been forgetting for the past three weeks. But if you wouldn't mind reminding me, I'd really like to do this.'"

And you know what? That made sense. That did sound more like a relationship. Like what you would say to a close friend: "Hey, don't let me forget, I need to make that phone call this afternoon." Or "Remind me when we get home to take the roast out of the freezer."

> Making a list is *religion,* not *relationship.*

So driving home, I asked the Lord to remind me. And guess what? Every morning that week, I'd be driving in my car, or putting in a load of laundry, or blow-drying my hair, and suddenly there it would be, in my head, the reminder that I wanted to pray. *Somebody's* memory seemed to be working fine. It just didn't happen to be mine.

An Encouraging Word

One day my friend Jeanette and I were talking about all this stuff. Before I tell you what we said, however, let me say that our friendship had begun in a rather inauspicious fashion eighteen months earlier, when I was in the absolute worst place of my emotional/spiritual/marital crisis. One Sunday I quietly slipped out of my Sunday school class hoping everyone would think I had to go to the bathroom, but the truth is that I felt like exploding from all the hurt and anger and confusion boiling around inside of me.

Even though she only knew me as an acquaintance, Jeanette could see that something was wrong. She slipped out of the class-room and caught up with me in the ladies' room. She asked if I needed to talk to someone. I said everything was fine. She said she knew I was suffering. I said, Nah, just a stressful time in my marriage. She said God wasn't through with my marriage yet. I literally grabbed my hair and pulled it hard and screamed, "You don't understand! I'm done! I'm doodly done!" Of course, I didn't say doodly. I said another word, the kind of word that will land a teenager on restriction for a month. And Jeanette just smiled. And when she went home, she prayed for me. And that's how I met Jeanette.

> I took those words and hid them in my heart. And on the days I felt like giving up on everything—my marriage, my God, and my sanity—I took them out and held them like amethysts and looked at their fire, and I knew I would be okay.

Eighteen months later, we were fast friends. We were talking about my crazy life in general and my crisis of faith specifically, when suddenly she mentioned her husband and said, "Remember when David came to your Max Lucado study a few times? Back when you weren't even sure God existed, but you showed up anyway and just kept asking questions and expressing your doubts?"

I nodded.

"One night he came home and looked at me and said, 'I listened to her talk tonight. I know she's struggling. I know she's in trouble. But she's not going down.'"

I took those words and hid them in my heart. And on the days I felt like giving up on everything—my marriage, my God, and my sanity—I took them out and held them like amethysts and looked at their fire, and I knew I would be okay. Not because I could see the light in myself but because some-one else had seen it in me.

Four Words God Hates to Hear

Several months later I visited a church in Beaver Creek, Colorado, and by the time I walked out of that little chapel in the woods, I was shaking my head. The pastor might have been holding a microphone and facing sixty people, but he'd been speaking just to me.

He'd said, "Last week I was working on the sermon for this morning when I realized *I* needed to work on the very things I was going to be talking about today. So I said, 'God, I'm going to do my best this week to live up to what I'm preaching.'"

I don't remember what the topic was that Sunday—maybe it was hearing the voice of the Holy Spirit, or controlling anger, or fleeing lust; I don't know. Whatever it was, the preacher before me had just spent seven days doing his best to live up to God's standards.

Had he succeeded?

I inched closer to the edge of my seat.

He took a deep breath and said, "The truth is, this has been one of the worst weeks of my life. Old temptations came back into my life. I blew it at every turn. And I couldn't believe it! Here I was trying so hard. And by the end of the week, I finally heard what God had been trying to say to me all along. God was telling me that those four little words—*I'll do my best*—are four of his least favorite words in the universe. Because he already knows that our best won't be good enough. It can never be good enough. Only his best can cut the mustard. Only his best is good enough. And we can only let him perform *his* best through us when we sit still and stop trying to impress him with *our* best."

I left the chapel feeling like the very air around me was brighter and clearer than it had ever been before. Maybe it was the Rocky Mountain air and all that. But I didn't think so. A sort of simmering shimmer permeated everything as well. I looked down at my sweater. Even my sweater looked different. I looked at the couple attending the service with us. Did they feel the magic too? I said, "Wow." Everyone else nodded and said, "Yes, it was a very good service." And I came to the conclusion that, nope, it was just me.

I knew what I'd heard that morning was the truth. The preacher had put into words something I'd known all along but was having a hard time accepting. My best would *never* be good enough. I'd thought this would be news to God. I'd imagined him up there saying, "What a devastating turn of events! I'm flabbergasted. Someone alert the media!"

> A sort of simmering shimmer permeated everything. I looked down at my sweater. Even my sweater looked different.

Now a different image came to mind: God chuckling and saying, "So you're not perfect? So you need me in your life to love, forgive, and empower you and, when you fall short even then, to love and forgive you some more? Oh, Karen, that's what I've been trying to tell you all along!"

I Can See Clearly Now

Several months ago Larry and I spent four days at a luxury hotel. He was there on business, and I got to go along just for fun.

The morning we packed up to head home, I was standing at the sink in the hotel bedroom, putting my contacts in, when I dropped one of the little suckers.

I searched the sink, the countertop, my clothes, the tops and sides of my shoes, the carpet around my feet, even my eyelashes. Larry helped too, but the contact was nowhere to be found.

I didn't have a spare. I sighed at the thought of the time and money it would take to get a new pair of contacts. I just hate it when I do this.

I remembered back to all the times I've dropped contact lenses in the past. I can't tell you how many times I've been unable to find a dropped lens, breathed a prayer to the Lord to help me find the silly thing, and then spotted it on my chest or eyelash or toothbrush.

Standing at the sink in that hotel room, I thought about those prayers. I thought, "I could do that again. I could pray right now." But I knew I didn't have the faith this time. Sure, I believed in God. Yes, I was learning that it was okay to admit that he's God and I'm not. But for some reason, I just didn't have the faith anymore to believe that he was present enough in my life to help me find a stupid missing contact lens.

The Bible says faith can move mountains. But what if you're plumb out of faith and the mountain moves anyway?

But I had nothing to lose. I didn't even close my eyes. I simply said in a dishrag voice, "Lord, I've got to be honest with you here. I don't have an ounce of faith. Not a drop. Not a mustard seed. Not even a molecule. But I'm saying the words anyway. Please help me find that lens. Amen."

I remembered I needed to brush my teeth. I walked four feet from the bedroom vanity to the bathroom. The moment my left foot went from carpet to tile, I heard the tiniest noise. The kind of noise the plastic tip of a shoelace makes against a hard surface. I looked down. I wasn't wearing any shoelaces. I stepped backwards and swept the floor with my eyes.

I saw my contact.

It had fallen off my shoe. Or maybe from heaven. I picked it up, washed it off, and popped it in.

I walked back into the bedroom and sat on the bed.

He's here. He's really here. In this room. With me. Loving me enough to answer even a pathetically faithless prayer.

The Bible says faith can move mountains. But what if you're plumb out of faith and the mountain moves anyway?

I looked at an empty chair in the corner. I imagined him sitting there, grinning at me. No vague ceiling-bound mutterings for me. I knew he was a lot closer than that.

128

I looked into his eyes.

"Thank you," I said, my own filling with hot tears. "Really. I mean it from the bottom of my heart. Thank you. For everything."

Pray with Joy

"I always pray with joy, being confident that he who began a good work in you will carry it on to completion until the day of Christ Jesus" (Phil. 1:4–6 NIV).

It feels weird, after forty years of loving God, to find myself reframing the whole thing, relearning the basics, rethinking my approach to God and his response to me.

In a way, when I think back over this past year, I can see that he's been wooing me, tenderly, patiently, the way you might pursue the heart of something wounded or skittish.

Several years ago, after I wrote *Just Hand Over the Chocolate and No One Will Get Hurt*, a woman reviewing my book wrote something along the lines—and I'm paraphrasing here—"Linamen wrote a little too much about 'falling in love with Jesus' and not enough about Jesus loving us for my personal taste."

I've thought about her comment off and on over the years. The chapter to which she referred was, indeed, about how you and I can fall deeper in love with Jesus. And what's so wrong with that? Nothing. Nothing at all.

Still . . . I had to admit it was merely one side of the coin. The other side of the coin was Jesus' great love for us. Why *hadn't* I written more about that?

Three years later, I can't *not* write about it. This is because, in the past thirty-six months, I've learned more about his love for me than in the previous four hundred and fifty-six combined.

And I'm still learning, still figuring out how to lose my religion and embrace a vibrant relationship with Jesus Christ in its place.

What about you?

What do you have in your life? It's possible that what you have is religion: a belief in God plus a list of do's, don'ts, and should's that gets you through your life.

And maybe that works for you.

Religion is great. It's fine. It gives guidance, inspiration, values, and community. It feeds the spirit. And when life's storms hit, religion gives something to hang on to, after all. The thing religion can't do, however, is hang on to you.

It takes a Person to do that.

And maybe that's what the Lord's been showing me after all.

One day, while I was still in the middle of all these experiences, I sat down and wrote a letter to Jeanette. It was about all this stuff we've just been talking about. And when it came time to end my letter, this is what I said:

> I'm never quite sure how to sign off on letters, but I saw this phrase used once to end a letter and even title a book and—even though I've never used it before myself—it seems fitting to use it now.
>
> But before I do, I need to tell you something. This past year, I've only been able to pray *one* prayer, and this is what it's been: "Lord, I should be hanging on to you, but I'm not. The truth is that I'm filled with doubts, and I feel so angry and wounded and rebellious it's like I can't even think straight. So I'm not holding on to you right now. No use beating around the bush; we both know it's true. But Lord, please, hold on to me. That's all I can ask. Please don't let me go. Just hold on to me and see me through this. Just hang on, okay? Hang on to me."
>
> I've prayed that prayer many times. And I'm beginning to think that, maybe, just maybe, he's in the process of doing just that. So perhaps I'll take that phrase after all, the phrase I've seen other people use, and go ahead and use it here . . .

And I signed my letter, "In his grip."

Easy Does It

I'm going to simplify my life, and I think you should too.

So here are a few of my goals: I'm going to schedule mammograms once a year and eat chocolate when it calls my name. I might even stop turning the launch of every diet into a national event and try, instead, the simple act of putting healthier foods into my mouth.

And when it comes to my soul, I've decided to stop making things more complicated than they need to be. I think I'll stop saying "I SHOULD . . ." and start admitting, "Lord, I can't . . . would you?" And I'll definitely keep talking to him, even when my faith is flatlining. I'd also like to keep thinking of him sitting as close as the chair next to mine, and even ask him to remind me of things too important to forget, just like I do with my very closest friends. And I'm going to let him hang on to me, even when I'm too weak to hang on to him.

In other words, I'm going to lose my religion—and ask the Lord to teach me what a relationship with him *really* looks like instead.

Care to join me?

12

....

Take the Hundred-Smile Challenge

B eth is not only a very good kidnapper, she makes a mean
casserole to boot.

One day she dropped by to cheer me up. She brought
with her this heavenly casserole. I mean, this casserole
was amazing. It had tons of cheese and sliced eggplant and
some eggs and tons of cream, and it had this Mediterranean-
flavor thing happening, and it just melted in your mouth, and
it was truly wonderful.

I get sort of passionate about food, if you hadn't noticed.

Anyway, so Beth shows up on my doorstep, and I make us
some coffee, and we dig into her casserole, and we spend several hours just talking about life in general and my life in particular. It was nothing short of a Kodak moment, all the
encouraging and bonding and feasting that was occurring.

Early afternoon, I walked her to the door. She paused on
my front porch, and our conversation began meandering

toward good-byes. We chatted casually about nothing in particular, when suddenly I announced, "I'm going to make it."

Beth said, "I KNOW you're going to make it. You're strong. You're a wonderful person, and you've gone through some tough times but, yes, you're going to make it. And I'm going to be there with you every step of the way. No matter what the future holds, no matter what decisions you make with your life, I love you and I'll be there for you. You're going to be okay, Karen. This year is going to be a new chapter in your life. You're going to be fine. You really ARE going to make it."

You don't have to be a rocket scientist to make someone's day.

By now there were tears in her eyes.

I blinked. I stared. Then I said, "I meant the casserole."

"The casserole?"

"I meant I'm going to make your casserole."

We got a good laugh out of the incident. But the truth remains that Beth's cooking and her empathy were the perfect combination of ingredients to raise my spirits and put a smile on my face.

And you know what? When it was all said and done, I wasn't the only one with lifted spirits. Beth felt great about what she'd done as well.

In my book *Just Hand Over the Chocolate and No One Will Get Hurt,* I included a chapter titled "Borrow a Whine." In it, I suggested that, when we're frustrated with long-term, seemingly unsolvable problems in our own lives, we turn our attentions outward, find someone with a problem we *can* solve, and hop to it.

Which is still a great idea.

But what if you and I decided to be a little more intentional about it? What if we actually made a plan? What if, when it came to bringing smiles to the faces of those around us, we gave ourselves a goal? An agenda? A quota even?

What if we attempted to bring smiles to the faces of LOTS of people in a limited period of time?

What if we took the Hundred-Smile Challenge?

Do-Gooding for Dummies

You don't have to be a rocket scientist to make someone's day. You also don't have to be a philanthropist or even a Mother Teresa wannabe. You don't even have to be 100 percent selfless because, let's be honest, do-gooding is bound to reap benefits for you as well. After all, would you rather be in the presence of one hundred *smiling* people or one hundred people who look like they're wearing thong underwear for the very first time?

You get my drift.

Plus there's that great thing that happens inside you and me when we've done a good deed. Sometimes it feels like a warm, fuzzy glow. Other times it feels like when you're supposed to be quiet—like in church or at a funeral—and you get this irrepressible urge to giggle and you have to stuff it down and enjoy that giggle deep down inside where no one really knows it's there. Other times it feels deeply satisfying, sort of like a really long hug from someone with whom you've always felt loved and at peace, regardless of anything else that was going on in your life at the time.

I LOVE to do good deeds for folks. I THRIVE on it. In fact, I make it a point to be engaged in some act of kindness for someone else whenever the idea crosses my mind *and* I

I make it a point to be engaged in some act of kindness for someone else whenever the idea crosses my mind *and* I happen to have spare time on my hands *and* I'm not completely self-absorbed by my own problems *and* it's the first Tuesday of the second week of the fifth month in an even-numbered year *and* I am not currently PMSing or having a bad hair day.

happen to have spare time on my hands *and* I'm not completely self-absorbed by my own problems *and* it's the first Tuesday of the second week of the fifth month in an even-numbered year *and* I am not currently PMSing or having a bad hair day.

But I'm wondering if maybe I can't do just a bit better than that.

You know, there are some things in life that feel so good that, once you've done them, you find yourself thinking, *Wow! This feels great! Why in the world don't I do this more often?*

Working out at the gym falls into that category for me. So does tackling some unpleasant task I've been putting off for months and crossing it off my to-do list once and for all.

And so does making someone smile.

So here's my idea. I'm going to try it first, and then I want you to try it. Let's see what kind of positive energy it creates in the lives of folks around us, and in your life and mine as well. Ready? Here it is:

I'm going to make it a goal to do an unexpected kindness for someone in my life each and every day for the next one hundred days.

That's one hundred smiles. Two hundred, actually, if we count what'll be happening on my face.

Let's give it a go, shall we? I'm just getting started, but here's what's happened so far.

Day One: I cleaned my daughter's room. She's fifteen, and you can't see the floor for the clothes, or the bed for the magazines, or the desk for the makeup. And most days we do the typical mother/daughter dance wherein I ask her to clean her room and she says she will, and I ask her again the next day and she assures me that she will, and I beg her the following day and she promises that she will, and I yell at her the fourth day and she rolls her eyes and says of COURSE she'll clean it and she has NO IDEA why I can't just talk to her in a civilized tone, and I remind her again on the fifth day and . . . well, you get the idea.

But on this particular night I snuck in her room while she was taking a shower and put fresh sheets on her bed, hung up all her clothes, and even lit the candles on her nightstand. I didn't have to hurry because, as I've mentioned, she is a teenager, and her natural habitat happens to be the bathroom. When she takes a shower, entire rain forests are impacted for weeks. I figured I'd have enough time not only to hang up her clothes but also to add a second story to her room and maybe even give birth to a third child before she returned.

Sure enough, after draining a modest number of natural lakes and reservoirs, she emerged from the bathroom and headed for her room. I was in my bedroom reading when I heard the squeals of joy. She ran into my room and gave me a hug, and then she gushed, "I can't believe you did that! You have no idea how that makes me feel! When you make my bed and hang up my clothes, I feel like I'm a little girl again and I feel all warm inside and taken care of and it's wonderful!" And she hugged me again before leaving to enjoy her room.

Kaitlyn is a teenager, and her natural habitat happens to be the bathroom. When she takes a shower, entire rain forests are impacted for weeks.

Day Two: I put a card in the mail to a girlfriend who is going through a tough time. I even added a few chocolate kisses. By the time they go through the mail they'll probably look more like chocolate quarters, but she'll get the idea.

Day Three: I wrote an e-mail to my sister. But instead of the usual, this time I wrote five paragraphs telling her how amazing and special she is. I told her what she has meant in my life and how much I rely on her strength and wisdom and what a lifeline she is to me.

Day Four: Okay, I can't take any credit for this one, but it's so good I'm going to tell you anyway. This afternoon my daughters, sister, mom, and I met up with my dad at Cracker Barrel for lunch. Our waiter was just a young kid. But what he lacked in experience and finesse he made up for with earnestness, if that's even a word. After we left the restaurant, my dad said, "While I was waiting for you girls to arrive, that kid must have asked me a dozen times if I wanted water or coffee or biscuits. I decided to make his day. I left him a twenty-dollar tip and, on the way out, told his manager what a good job he'd done."

Day Five: Today's a busy day. It has to be something quick. While packing Kacie's lunch, I decorated her paper napkin with a picture of a frog under a speech bubble. The frog is saying: "I'd hop a mile to tell you what a special girl you are!"

Day Six: Kacie and I made chocolate chip cookies—only *slightly* burned regardless of what you may have heard—and delivered them to several neighbors. Kacie thought this was so much fun, the next day she picked flowers—okay, so they were weeds—and took them to the same families. If we keep this up, before long there'll be "For Sale" signs up and down my street.

My grandmother talks about naked people who come into her room and eat peanuts. Apparently this would be fine with Mamaw if they didn't leave shells all over her carpet.

Day Seven: I called my eighty-seven-year-old grandma at the nursing home, and we had a nice long chat. This is always an adventure. Sometimes she talks about family members, or about Jesus and what he's meant to her through the years, or about how she's ready to go to heaven and be with loved ones. Other times she talks about naked people who come into her room and eat peanuts. Apparently this would be fine with Mamaw if they didn't leave shells all over her carpet.

Day Eight: When I packed Kacie off to school, I sent a little something for her teacher—a copy of my book *Welcome to the Funny Farm* along with a thank-you note for the role she plays in Kacie's life.

Day Nine: Several weeks ago I asked Kacie what I do that really makes her feel like I love her. For example, I tell her that

I love her several times a day. I also often invite her to bring a book and cuddle on my lap for a story. I wondered if those things made her feel loved. She said no. Actually, the thing that makes her feel most loved is when I eat popcorn and watch a movie with her. So on day nine I filled the biggest bowl I could find with popcorn, and Kacie and I snuggled down to watch *Miss Congeniality*.

Day Ten: A friend of mine is struggling with chronic pain, so I drew funny pictures on five index cards. I addressed them and stamped them and set them by the door. I mailed one card every day for a week.

Day Eleven: My totally stressed sister asked me if I would babysit her eighteen-month-old daughter while she and her husband enjoyed a much overdue date night. I said sure. That morning, I drove to Wal-Mart and bought candy, flowers, snacks, candles, a bottle of sparkling grape juice, and two plastic cups shaped like wine glasses. I drove to a local motel and paid for a room, then stocked it with all the goodies. After lunch I caught up with Shell and Russ at my folks' house, still several hours before their big "date" was scheduled to begin. Handing them the room key, I said, "Pack a bag and don't come back till morning." The whole thing cost me less than sixty bucks and was worth every penny.

> I paid a compliment to a total stranger working in a pizza parlor. And in about three years, when I'm sure he's found another job, I can start buying pizza there again.

Day Twelve: Still mailing those homemade postcards. On day twelve I also paid a compliment to a total stranger working in a pizza parlor. I was picking up two large pizzas, and he was the guy wearing the spattered apron and handing the boxes over the counter. Average looking, fiftyish, thick around the middle, and a little tired-looking, he nevertheless had the most amazing eyes. Pretty. Beautiful even. Women would kill for lashes like his. I said, "You know, I'm TOTALLY married, and

I'm NOT hitting on you, but I wanted to tell you that you've got gorgeous eyes." He lit up like high beams on a Mack truck. And in about three years, when I'm sure he's found another job, I can start buying pizza there again.

Day Thirteen: I sent an e-mail greeting card to my friend Cherie. It said, "I tried to take up jogging but my thighs rubbed together so bad they set my panty hose on fire."

Day Fourteen: Today I was next in line at the cashier's station at Target when the young woman in front of me realized she was a few dollars short. She was deciding which item to delete from her tab when I handed her a five. When she promised to send me a check, I said, "Forget it. I run short in cashier's lines all the time." And the sad thing is, it's true. I do.

Day Fifteen: I gave my friend Nancy fourteen chickens and a rooster. For no reason other than to brighten her day. And because Nancy lives in the city and the LAST thing she needs is a harem of chickens in her living room, her chickens are being tended by a grateful family in Haiti. Nancy only had to take possession of a gift card. It was mailed to her by World Vision, and it informed her that a third world family had been given chickens in her honor. If you would like to brighten someone's day by providing a gift of chickens to a third-world family, call World Vision at 1-888-511-6511 (or visit them on the web at www.worldvision.org). And because chickens are not necessarily a one-size-fits-all gift, World Vision has made it possible for you to also give goats.

I'm a little more than two weeks into this experiment, and I have to admit, I'm having fun. I'm not sure I can come up with one hundred *new* ideas, however, so I'm already planning on some repeats. For example, greeting cards, e-mails, phone

> Because Nancy lives in the city and the LAST thing she needs is a harem of chickens in her living room, her chickens are being tended by a grateful family in Haiti.

Inspiration for Do-Gooders

Need some ideas? The Random Acts of Kindness Foundation was founded in 1995 as a resource for groups and individuals who want to spread kindness. The foundation provides leadership, educational, and promotional materials as well as opportunities for folks to get involved with projects and events designed to promote kindness. You can check out their web site at www.actsofkindness.org. You'll find personal stories and quotes, as well as research on the health benefits of performing kindnesses. (What kinds of benefits? How about less stress; a stronger immune system; and a decrease in depression, physical pain, and even obesity!). You'll even find ideas of kind things you can do.

calls, and even chickens can be given to many people in my life. I also think it will be fun, in the coming weeks, to expand my circle of influence. So far I've done a few nice things for strangers, but most of my deeds have benefited close friends and family. I'd like to come up with more ideas that impact total strangers. I'll let you know how it goes.

And it's not like I'm not getting something out of it. In addition to this sort of bright yellow feeling inside, I'm reaping boomerang benefits as well. Last week, after a particularly tiresome day, I emerged from the shower with one thing on my mind: to climb into bed and turn out the lights. Approaching my bed, I spotted a cup of steaming tea and an encouraging note from Kaitlyn.

Which gives me a sneaky idea. If Kaitlyn's going to catch on to this "do-gooding" stuff, I think I'll have Beth show her how to make that casserole.

13

Break Out of Solitary Confinement

Papaw was a character. I don't think I ever saw him without a twinkle in his eye. Except maybe at the end, when Alzheimer's betrayed him into doing things like holding his eyeglasses in his hands, looking at his reflection in the mirrored closet doors, and saying fretfully, "That man won't give me back my glasses." Okay, sure. Sometimes then the twinkle waned, but for all the years before that, the twinkle was standard Papaw, as standard as his fastidiously trimmed mustache.

I think the twinkle is the reason he got away with so much. Like the nicknames he gave everyone. I don't think I ever heard Papaw call a single person by their names given at birth. My grandmother was ever and only "Baby-doll." He called my dad "Spud." He called my mom "Sweetie." His daughter, Jeanette, was dubbed "Trick."

He called his grandson "Gabe," even though Gabe's name was actually Michael. My sister Renee became "Reenie Bird," Papaw called me "Moog," and Michelle—don't ask me why—was known as "Pete." And my cousin Kerri—heaven help her—answered to "Deedoo" long after she married.

I think the twinkle also made it possible for Papaw to get away with the whole dessert thing. As a kid, I envied and admired my grandpa for what he was able to accomplish at the dinner table. He'd start with, say, pie and ice cream. He'd polish off the ice cream, then say, "I might as well have a little more ice cream to finish off these last few bites of pie." Naturally, he'd have enough ice cream left over that he'd need another half a piece of pie, which caused him, inevitably, to require just one more dab of ice cream ...

This would go on longer than you might think. Eventually, his sweet tooth sated, he would polish off his plate with a final forkful of caloric bliss, a perfectly balanced arrangement of gastronomical delights both frozen and baked.

Some things are better off by themselves. Apparently pie is not on the list.

Know what else needs company? Chocolate. One piece of chocolate is simply criminal. This is why they package chocolate in boxes, for crying out loud, so every piece has some company. As far as I'm concerned, the only time chocolate should be associated with the number "one" is when you are talking about the number of servings in a two-pound box. Of course, this explains why, in my experience, they're making "one size fits all" a little snug these days.

> As far as I'm concerned, the only time chocolate should be associated with the number "one" is when you are talking about the number of servings in a two-pound box.

I can think of many other things that are sociable by nature. A good belly laugh comes to mind. I'm not saying that a belly laugh absolutely can't exist by itself, but this kind of gregarious guffaw typically prefers to travel in crowds of two or more.

You know what else was never intended to be alone?

You and me.

According to the Book of Genesis, God set the record straight on this subject from the start. He looked at Adam and said, "It is not good for man to be alone." He gave Adam pets, then a wife, then relatives, and eventually—as the population grew and the bloodline thinned out enough so that every marriage wasn't between cousins—even friends.

I write about the value and power of friends all the time. As a result, women write back to me about their friendships.

Fancy Meeting You Here!

Michelle says when she was single and lonely for friends, her philosophy was to never turn anything—NOT ONE THING—down. She says, "It didn't matter if someone invited me to a Tupperware party, New Year's Eve gathering, women's retreat, Chamber of Commerce breakfast, craft class or scrapbooking thing, neighborhood progressive dinner, or garage sale. I was there."

If you have kids or a husband, you won't have the same freedom, but the principle is a sound one. As often as possible, accept invitations, attend functions, get out of the house and in the path of potential friends. Where can you and I meet potential friends? Here are some ideas:

◎ Check your city's web site for festivities and functions.

◎ Meet your neighbors. Last week Kacie, Kaitlyn, and I took small plates of macaroni salad to the homes of four of our neighbors. Cherie and Lynn hosted a neighborhood tea. Michelle invited two families who live on her street to her home for dinner.

◎ Join a MOPS group for mothers of preschoolers or start a play group.

◎ Get to know moms of your kids' classmates and playmates.

◎ Check out a women's Bible study at your church or at any church near your home.

They write to me about their best friends, sisters, and moms. Sometimes they ask for advice regarding their relationships. Sometimes they tell me a funny story. Sometimes they tell me that a friend or sister is going through a tough time—maybe she can't bear children, or has been diagnosed with breast cancer, or is going through a divorce—and ask what they can do to be an encouragement. One reader wrote to me about the recent death of her mom and how much she missed the love, wisdom, and company of this remarkable woman.

Sometimes, however, women write to me and say, "I don't have the kind of friends you write about, and I'm so hungry for friendship I can barely stand it!"

There are many reasons why a woman may be experiencing a shortage of friends. She might feel isolated because she lives way out in the boondocks or because of a recent move to a new city. She might feel isolated due to shyness, illness, depression, divorce, or even her own tendency to keep people at arm's length. Misunderstandings and typecasting might have something to do with it, as in the case of the woman who told me that her love of blue jeans and Harleys makes it hard for her to be embraced by the society ladies in her small Southern town.

Can we find friends in the Yellow Pages? Is there a particular perfume, dental floss, or floor wax that can guarantee friends by the dozen or we get our money back?

Sometimes a woman feels lonely because her bosom buddy—her best friend in all the world—moved away, moved to heaven, or became a casualty in a feud between friends.

People assume that just because I write about my friends all the time that I am a stranger to the politics of loneliness and the bittersweet process of trying to make new friends.

Not so.

There have been many seasons in my life when I have found myself alone and lonely and hungering for connection.

Take right now, for instance.

Two summers ago three families who were like family to me moved away and left a huge void in my heart and social calendar. The Spurlocks, Cleggs, and Rottmeyers. Thank God that Beth, Darla, Belinda, Diane, Jeanette and a few others were still within shoutin' distance.

Last summer, I was the one who climbed into a U-Haul and drove off into the sunset. Luckily for me, three of my best friends live an hour away—my sister, mom, and, yes, even Cherie Spurlock, who made the trek from Texas to Colorado before I did.

I see them as often as I can despite the long drive. But in the daily scheme of things, I'm starting over. New neighborhood. New church. New supermarket, dry cleaners, and hair salon.

No one drops by my house unexpectedly anymore. No one calls me and says, "Wanna go for coffee?" No one offers to run errands together. No familiar faces or hugs greet me when I walk into the sanctuary on Sunday, and there's no one to go to lunch with after the sermon's done.

That's not how I like to live.

So, what can I do about it? Can I create new and meaningful connections in my daily world? Can you? If so, how do we go about it? Is there a scientific formula, magic potion, or 1-800 number that will help? Can we find friends in the Yellow Pages? Is there a particular perfume, dental floss, or floor wax that can guarantee friends by the dozen or we get our money back?

For this topic, I decided to call in the experts. I called five women I know who, like me, have recently relocated and are starting from scratch on the friendometer. Then I picked their brains to find out just how they're doing it. I figured I just might learn a thing or two, and maybe you will too.

Fido Is the Ticket

Geri Scalf is my mom. Southern California was her home her entire life, as well as the home of her parents and grandparents. She had roots in the community before she was even born. She recently moved to Colorado, and when I asked her about the art of making friends, one of the suggestions she gave me was: Get a dog!

"When you have a dog with you, everyone is your friend. In the park, neighborhood, or even just across the backyard fence, everyone wants to stop and visit and play with your furry friend. When I had my little dog, Buddy, people stopped me to talk all the time. In fact, the same woman stopped by

One Woman's Story of Success!

I loved getting this letter from a reader:

> Dear Karen,
> I am on chapter 11 of your book *Just Hand Over the Chocolate and No One Will Get Hurt.* To make a long story short, it made me realize that I needed TRUE friends. It's not that I'm a loner, but I don't have a lot of time, and in the past I've had some friends who have pulled me down rather than lifted me up, so I figured I was better on my own. Boy, was I wrong!
>
> After reading your book, I tried to make friends in my son's day care at church, but they were busy picking up their kids and didn't have time for me.
>
> I forgot one important thing: God. I hadn't prayed about it. One day I asked him, "Lord, what kind of friends do you want me to have?" The answer came that Sunday. Our pastor was talking about getting God off the shelf and into your life. As a result, I started to attend the Women's Ministries Bible study where we are talking about becoming a woman of grace. It has only been three weeks and I have already found a GROUP of friends!
>
> Instead of me trying to find just one friend on my own, I handed it off to God and let him do his work, and he brought me into a whole group of women who are just absolutely fabulous! The Lord is so good!

148

every day to play with him through the fence. I enjoyed her visits as well!"

You Can Walk a Long Way on a Little Common Ground

Four weeks after moving from Texas to Colorado, Cherie Spurlock met one of her neighbors. Lynn asked, "Do you like to walk?"

Cherie said, "I used to walk every day."

Lynn said, "Great! Let's go!"

They met the following day at 9:00 A.M. for a two-mile hike around their hilly neighborhood. That was two years ago, and they're still footin' it. Cherie says, "We started slow. Lynn was patient with my inability to function at this higher altitude, but she made sure we walked every day, rain, shine, or snow. She's from Chicago, after all. One morning she phoned and said, 'Are you ready?' I said, 'No way! It's too cold!' She said, 'Put on another layer. I'll be there in ten minutes.'"

The common ground they shared soon led to other things.

They had been walking together for six weeks when Cherie said, "I don't know anyone in this neighborhood besides you. Let's plan a neighborhood tea." Eighteen women came. Lynn and Cherie served strawberry bread, scones, tea, fruit, chocolate-dipped strawberries, and plenty of smiles. On that day, friendships were forged that are still going strong.

Just like Lynn's and Cherie's. Cherie says, "We do joint runs to Sam's, Marshall's, and Ross. She helps me with interior decorating, and I bake cookies for her family. They just closed our favorite Chinese place, which was traumatic, but I shouldn't complain. I'm sure we'll have fun finding a new 'favorite' spot to go!"

> They met the following day at 9:00 A.M. for a two-mile hike around their hilly neighborhood. That was two years ago, and they're still footin' it.

And to think—it all started when Lynn asked a simple question that got the friendship off on the right foot, in more ways than one!

Reaping the Benefits of Volunteering

Shortly after moving from California to Colorado, Jeanette Sharp (aka "Trick") read a newspaper article about a man who volunteered at a local hospital rocking premature or sick babies. Before you could say "Gitchy-gitchy-goo," Trick had picked up the phone, called the hospital, and arranged an interview with the volunteer coordinator.

To Michelle, everyone is a best friend until proven otherwise. As a result, she never meets a stranger.

Trick says, "I saw it as an enjoyable way to get out of my house." With a six-month waiting list to cuddle newborns, she looked into volunteer opportunities in other departments. Every Tuesday morning, she runs the volunteer gift boutique. Every Wednesday, she screens the hearing of newborn babies.

She says, "When you don't have friends, it's easy to find yourself sitting at home twiddling your thumbs. Sometimes you have to be creative to find ways to break out of the isolation and connect. I get a lot out of my volunteer work each week. It's a way to meet new people, and I always feel like I've done something worthwhile at the end of the day."

There's No Place like Home

Nancy Rottmeyer moved to Fort Wayne, Indiana, last year. Eighteen months later, Nancy has yet to replace the kind of friendships she left in Texas.

Some things just take time.

She says, "Part of it is where I live. A lot of people went to school here, graduated here, have their extended families here—and they don't have a lot of need for other friendships, like the woman who told us, 'I pretty much socialize with my family.' That's common. So it's been tough."

Nancy says there are three things that usually work well for her when she wants to make new friends: (1) attending women's Bible studies at church; (2) selecting a smallish church of a couple hundred people, rather than a megachurch; and (3) inviting people to her home for dinner, card games, dessert, or even tea. "Having people over to the house is a big thing. There's something personal about that, if you can get to someone's house rather than just to a restaurant or movie. In Texas we frequently had people over for cards and games or Sunday meals or Friday night dessert or whatever."

"I ask tons of questions, like when you have a best friend and you've been separated for weeks, and you want to catch up on every little detail. Because that's what we women want to talk about anyway, the details in our lives."

Reflecting on the four years her family lived in Texas, Nancy says, "I haven't replaced those friendships. I look back on those times in Texas and know they were special. And it wasn't because we went out for fancy meals or big organized events. It was because we spent time in each other's homes."

The good news is that Nancy says there is a couple in her Sunday school class that she and her husband are starting to make a connection with. In fact, the two families are having dinner together in a few weeks. Nancy just moved into a new house closer to her kids' school and is starting to meet her new neighbors. And she and her husband have already talked about inviting people into their home more often to play games and have dessert.

Yep, some goals just take time. But that doesn't mean they aren't worth the wait.

You're Cooking Now!

Here's the menu that helped Lynn and Cherie make their neighborhood tea such a success:

Chocolate Dipped Strawberries
English Scones (recipe follows)
Mock Devonshire Cream (recipe follows)
Strawberry Nut Bread (recipe follows)
And of course . . . tea!

English Scones

Mix together the following dry ingredients:
  2 cups flour
  1 tablespoon baking power
 1/2 teaspoon salt

Using a pastry blender, a fork, or 2 knives, cut in the following until it looks like coarse cornmeal:
6 tablespoons butter (not margarine)

Make a well in the center of the mixture and stir in the following until the dough clings together and is sticky—do not overmix:
1/2 cup buttermilk

Turn dough onto a floured surface and shape into an 8 inch round that is about 1 1/2 inches thick. Quickly cut into circles using a large biscuit cutter. Place on an ungreased cookie sheet, making sure the sides of the scones do not touch. Brush each scone with lightly beaten egg. Bake at 400 degrees for 10–15 minutes or until golden brown—not too dark!

Try to handle the dough as little as possible. This is the key to making tender scones. You may also add cinnamon, cut up fruit (apples, apricots, blueberries, etc.), or even chocolate chips. I like to make them plain and top with homemade preserves, clotted cream, or lemon curd.

Mock Devonshire Cream
Half sour cream
Half cream cheese
Powdered sugar to taste

Strawberry Nut Bread
Sift together into a large mixing bowl:
3 cups flour
1 teaspoon soda
1 teaspoon salt
1 tablespoon cinnamon
2 cups sugar

Make a well in the center and set aside.

Combine the following, mixing well:
4 eggs, beaten
1 1/4 cups vegetable oil
2 cups (16 oz.) thawed frozen sliced strawberries
1 1/4 cups chopped pecans

Pour the liquid mixture into the well of the dry ingredients—stirring just enough to moisten the dry mixture. Pour into 5 or 6 greased 6x3x2 inch pans or 2 greased 9x5x3 inch pans. Bake at 350 degrees—40 minutes for small pans and 1 hour for large pans. Remove from oven and let cool 5 minutes before removing from pans.

Assume the Best

Michelle Willett just moved from California to Monument, Colorado. Her secret for turning a new face into a close friend is simple: She pretends they are already bosom buddies.

"People say to me all the time, 'It's like you're my family!' or 'I feel like I've known you forever!'"

Michelle's explanation? "When I meet a woman at a Bible study, PTA meeting, banquet, tea, or wherever, I automatically assume that she is fun and that she's going to like me. I don't assume that there are walls of class, education, or attitude. I try to approach her without any negative judgments, games, insecurities, or that 'I wonder what she'll think of me!' kind of feeling! When you assume everyone is already your best friend—and treat them that way—it's easier to fall right into a good friendship."

You've heard the phrase "guilty until proven innocent"? Well, to Michelle, everyone is a best friend until proven otherwise. As a result, she never meets a stranger. And more times than not, her assumptions pan out into reality.

Fifteen Ways to Make a Friend!

Get a dog ☺ Exercise together ☺ Plan a neighborhood event ☺ Volunteer ☺ Attend a small group or women's Bible study ☺ Invite people to your home for dessert ☺ Consider attending a small fellowship rather than a mega church ☺ Assume the best about people you meet ☺ Be interested in the details of the lives of people around you ☺ Use memory tricks to remember the names of people you meet ☺ Befriend the friendless ☺ Strengthen bonds with friends you already have ☺ Never, never, never entertain critical words or thoughts about your friends ☺ Be a good listener ☺ Don't panic during dormant times in your social life—use the time to rest, reflect, or regroup.

So how does she treat strangers like best friends? She says, "I'm genuinely interested in them and in their life. Every person is interesting to me—it doesn't matter if she has ten degrees, or an earring in her nose, or lives in a trailer park with her eleven children, or wears a diamond ring on every finger. And I ask tons of questions. I get right to the nitty gritty: 'So are you married or do you have a boyfriend? Really, a boyfriend? So how's it going? Do you think there's a future? What do your parents think of him?' or 'So you're married? So how's it going? Is marriage different than what you thought?' I want to know what is going on in her life right now, like when you have a best friend and you've been separated for weeks, and you want to catch up on every little detail. Because that's what we women want to talk about anyway, the details in our lives."

Michelle adds, "I'm not ego-hungry. I don't have to have the spotlight. I don't mind giving the spotlight to a new friend. Trying to vie for the spotlight is pointless, because if you've done something to deserve the spotlight, it'll shine on you. I never compete with women. It's not about me trying to pump myself up. It's often about me trying to find out what their accomplishments and struggles and thoughts are. My stuff will come out at some point. I don't need to look for opportunities to shine. I am what I am, and whatever I am will show."

Friends Forever

Look for common ground (like animals or exercise!). . . . Spend time volunteering—it will get you out of the house and into the path of potential friends. . . . Attend women's Bible studies or retreats. . . . Invite people into your home. . . . Assume the best about someone you meet, then treat them as your dearest friend. . . .

I loved interviewing these women about this stuff. And I, for one, got some good ideas out of the exchange—I hope you did too!

Here are a few other thoughts:

◎ When meeting a new person, I use the old trick of saying her name at least three times during our conversation, so I can remember it later. And if I forget a name I try never to be embarrassed about it. The next time we meet I simply say, "I really enjoyed the last time we spoke, but I've forgotten your name." That works so much better than spending the next fifteen minutes trying to hide the fact that I've forgotten a name, or feeling paranoid that someone will join us and I'll have to make an introduction!

◎ The cure for loneliness isn't always to make new friends. We can also choose to strengthen and deepen bonds with people we already know.

◎ Don't only look for people you'd like to have as friends— also keep an eye out for women who might need a friend in you.

◎ I agree with Michelle when she says, "Don't be critical of other people. When you think and voice critical thoughts— 'So and so has terrible breath, or talks too much' or whatever—it changes the way you think about that person." And nix competitive words or cutting jokes. As Cicero wrote, "Never injure a friend, even in jest."

◎ Look for any connection, no matter how small it might seem. Friendship is a search for connection, a search to see what you have in common. Michelle met Tina when her church hosted a ladies' tea. Over scones, Tina said, "My husband just bought me a sewing machine for Christmas, but I don't know how to use it." Michelle said, "I know how to use a sewing machine. I'll come over and show you how." They've been friends ever since.

◎ Cherish any connection you find. You don't have to hit on every cylinder. One friend is good for boy talk, another for craft talk, another for problem-solving. One woman might be good company when you run errands, another is your garage-sale buddy, another is a wonderful prayer partner, and so on.

◎ Be a good listener. Use good nonverbals such as nodding or say "uh huh" to show your interest. Don't use everything she says as an opportunity to turn the conversation back to you.

◎ Be attentive to the goings-on in the life of your friends. Cherie is the queen when it comes to remembering birthdays and special occasions with cards or flowers. Michelle actually writes reminders in her calendar to call new friends once a week just to say hi and see how their life is going.

I wish I could say that friendship is a given, sort of like death and taxes. But the truth is, there are seasons in our lives when we find ourselves alone. These can be rich times as well, as we learn how to befriend ourselves. Sometimes we need these socially dormant seasons to rest, reflect, or regroup. Sometimes, in the quiet, we discover characteristics about ourselves, things we might not have known before, like the fact that we're pretty good company after all.

My wish for you is for friends, even during those seasons in your life when that friend turns out to be you.

And if you're ever in Colorado, look me up and we'll have lunch. There's a restaurant in Castle Rock I love. It's called Pegasus on the Square, and they've got great food, not to mention incredible desserts! We can even ask for seconds on the ice cream.

Papaw would have loved it there.

14

Forgive Yourself

Last week I drove to Westar Communications here in Colorado Springs; I was going to be a guest on *The Lynda Hunter Show*. Lynda had called and invited me. I think this is noteworthy because it's not every woman who is smart enough to get her own radio show.

I've worked with Lynda before. She is classy, beautiful, and talented, not to mention smart and sophisticated and witty. Did I mention that she is smart?

I want you to know all this about Lynda because of the story I'm about to tell you.

It has to do with the time Lynda got lost in a tanning booth.

It wasn't the bed kind of booth, but the stand-up kind. Sort of like a shower stall. I wish, for Lynda's sake, that I could say this was one of those maze-like shower-stall tanning booths that take up entire city blocks. Sometimes they go on for miles. Certainly you've heard of them. But it wasn't. It was one of the smaller variety. About two feet by two feet.

It happened like this: While tanning, Lynda twirled around to make sure she browned evenly (think of a marshmallow to the flame). When her seven minutes of tanning were up, Lynda went to open the door, unaware of the fact that she was now facing the wall. She groped and searched and pushed in vain. Then she began to pound and yell for help.

It's probably a good thing that the noise of fans and hairdryers drowned out her cries for help. Seems to me the LAST thing you want is for a locksmith, fireman, or tanning salon manager to come to your aid when you are naked, even if you *do* have nice color.

Eventually, Lynda found the door and escaped.

Sure, Lynda was embarrassed, but not nearly as embarrassed as the time she got both of her lips caught in the car door.

I didn't think it was physically possible either. But she swears it happened. And I believe her, because in addition to being smart, she is also honest. Did I mention that she has a doctorate?

I don't know why these things happen. But Lynda is a woman after my own heart, because these are the kinds of things that happen to me all the time. Daily, in fact. Like the time I drove over my husband's laptop computer with my car. Or the time I went through the car wash—without my car. Or the time a guest visited my home and, before she could go to the bathroom, she had to fish two wooden blocks and a set of car keys from the commode.

Things like this happen to my friends too. Like the day Beth called me and said, "I've left my purse at Foleys. I would drive there and pick it up, but I've also managed to lose my car keys. Can you come over?"

I drove to her house, and we spent the next hour ransacking her home looking for her keys. Unsuccessful, we decided to take my car to Foleys. We exited Beth's house through the garage so she could set the burglar alarm. As we walked around the side of the house to my car, Beth said, "You didn't happen to set the deadbolt on the front door, did you?"

I said, "Actually, I did."

Beth said, "I have to go back and unlock it, otherwise when Rachel gets home from school she won't be able to get into the house."

We retraced our steps to the back of Beth's house, where we discovered that she had forgotten to close the garage door. Thank goodness the burglar alarm had been set!

Whoops. It hadn't. Beth had forgotten to set the alarm as well.

We unbolted the front door, set the alarm, and closed the garage door.

I was chuckling to myself as we walked back to the front of the house where my car was waiting for us. Thank goodness at least *one* of us had a brain that morning.

> Ever do something stupid and you just can't let yourself forget it?

I stopped and stared.

My car door was hanging wide open, exactly where I'd flung it two hours ago on my way into Beth's house. The good news was that my purse was right where I'd left it.

It was on the roof of my car.

Comedy Is Merely Tragedy Plus Time

Sometimes the goofy things we do are good for a laugh. It might take a day or a decade, but eventually we can chuckle over past mistakes, ill-fated plans, and good intentions gone awry.

But sometimes we never laugh.

Sometimes we look back and wince, and the words that come to mind are, "If only . . ." and they are fueled by regret and conviction and maybe even angst.

Ever do that? Do something stupid and you just can't let yourself forget it?

I know a woman—I'll call her Annie—who is convinced that the man she married at the age of twenty-four was not the right choice for her. For years Annie couldn't look at a photo of herself in her twenties without feeling disgust and anger toward the young woman reflected there. In fact, most of the time she averted her eyes. Turned her head. Her grudge toward her younger self was so huge that she couldn't even look herself in the eye.

When we can't forgive—ourselves or someone else—we open a Pandora's box of ills.

Another friend—I'll call her Jill—has a secret. She won't tell me what it is. It's something she's done that she considers too horrible for words. In fact, she is so angry at herself that she punishes herself daily for her crime. She punishes herself with food. I know this, because one day she and I were talking about how hard it is to lose weight when she said, "I have a secret. It's something I've never told anyone. It's the thing that makes me unlovable. Sometimes I think that the day I tell someone my secret will be the day I stop abusing myself with food."

The truth is, when we can't forgive—ourselves or someone else—we open a Pandora's box of ills. Out of our unforgivingness springs a host of undesirables. These include bitterness, revenge, high blood pressure, hate, murder, slander, gossip, migraines, divorce, depression, and disillusionment. Sometimes, when we can't forgive, we find ourselves giving up and refusing to love again, or try again, or hope again. Unforgivingness can also pave the way for abuse and addictions—how many jilted lovers have let bitterness drive them to drink? Unforgivingness may even open the door for cancer, since some studies link emotional distress with not only a decrease in our bodies' immune system but also the development of rogue cells.

Yep, any number of these little goodies can be yours—when you can't forgive. And it doesn't matter if the person you can't forgive is your parent, your former best friend, your ex-husband, a total stranger, or yourself.

Feel like you're going crazy? Tired of hurting? Maybe you're not suffering from insanity as much as you are suffering from unforgivingness. And perhaps the mistake or wrongdoing you can't quite forgive is something that was done by . . . well, by you.

I've got a couple of these in my life as well, mistakes for which I'm still figuring out how to forgive myself. I don't have it all figured out yet, but here's what I've learned so far from my life and the lives of other women I know.

Spill the Beans

Like my friend with the binge-inducing secret, sometimes we need to find a trusted friend or professional and spill the beans before we can get on with the work of forgiving and forgetting.

Jill and I were sitting in a corner booth at Chili's the night she told me about her dark secret and the power it held over her. I tried in vain to get her to tell me what it was. She shook her head and said it was far too terrible.

> Feel like you're going crazy? Tired of hurting? Maybe you're not suffering from insanity as much as you are suffering from unforgivingness.

I fell silent for a while, thinking about what to say next. Finally, I looked across the table into her eyes and said quietly, "If you told me that you'd had an affair, this is what I would say to you. I would say 'Jill, I still love you and I forgive you.'"

She said, "It's not an affair."

I said, "And if you told me you'd had an abortion, this is what I would say to you. I would say, 'Jill, I still love you and I forgive you.'"

She said, "It's not an abortion."

I said, "And if you told me you were a bank robber . . ."

It took fifteen minutes, but I went through everything I could possibly think of. Tax evasion, polygamy, shoplifting, prescription drug abuse, pickpocketing, even taking store-bought food to a church potluck. According to Jill, I never named her secret. But it doesn't matter. I think I made my point. Which was that there was nothing she could do or think or say that would put her beyond the grasp of love or forgiveness.

Did I have the power to forgive Jill? Probably not, since I don't think her crime had been committed against me. My guess is that the person who needs to forgive Jill is Jill. And God, who is totally willing to do so if Jill merely asks him. And maybe a third party, depending on what in the world she did.

> Jill and I were sitting in a corner booth at Chili's the night she told me about her dark secret.

But I wanted to say the words anyway: "I forgive you." Because I hoped that if Jill could receive them from me, maybe she could receive them from herself as well.

Keep the Broth, Dump the Fat

There's something I regret in my life. I'll spare you the details, but I was hurting and angry and rebellious, and I acted out of all that pain. One night I was talking to my mom about it when she said, "Karen, keep the good. Toss the bad."

It made me think of cooking. Which is a strange connection for me because I never actually cook. My idea of a home-cooked meal is anything that requires three or more boxes, bags, or cans. By my definition, even a trip to McDonald's can be considered a homecooked meal if you insist on individual bags for your Big Mac, fries, and shake.

But I *used* to cook, back in those first years of marriage, back when TV reruns still featured housewives wearing dresses and pearls. Which means I still remember certain cooking

164

basics, like what to do with all that liquid left over after you boil a chicken.

What I remember is this: You wait until the liquid cools and the fat separates from the broth. Then you skim all that fat off the top and throw it away, leaving all that golden broth.

When I think back on most of my mistakes, I realize they're made up of both broth and fat. Sometimes I've got to cool my heels a bit, but by and by I'm able to separate the two. Then it's my choice as to what I toss and what I keep.

Sometimes I keep the fat.

Like when a relationship goes belly-up. Why is it easier to hang on to all those nasty feelings of rejection and toss the wonderful fact that you were loved by someone, even if it wasn't for as long as you would have liked?

I wonder if there are some mistakes so horrifying that no broth exists. I don't really know. I guess it's possible, although I can't think of any at the moment. The truth is, when I think about even my *worst* mistakes—and, trust me, I've made some doozies—looking back I can still find a little broth amid all the artery-hardening sludge.

Be Your Own Best Friend

Okay, here's one of my bonehead actions I can actually tell you about. I'm having a hard time forgiving myself for regaining twenty-seven of the sixty pounds I lost a couple years ago. Every time I look in the mirror—or have to bypass the sexy jeans I wore last summer for leggings and a tunic instead—I give myself a good tongue-lashing.

I'm an encourager by nature. When my girlfriends gain weight, make mistakes, struggle with depression, or feel like giving up on their dreams, I'm their biggest cheerleader.

But when I screw up, I turn into Eeyore on steroids.

So one day I started wondering what I would say to someone I really loved—a best girlfriend or sister—who had just packed on twenty-seven unwanted pounds. Would I berate or bless? Nag or nurture? Criticize or encourage?

I pretended I was my own best friend—instead of my own best accuser—and wrote myself a letter. And this is what I wrote:

My idea of a homecooked meal is anything that requires three or more boxes, bags, or cans. Even a trip to McDonald's can be considered a homecooked meal if you insist on individual bags for your Big Mac, fries, and shake.

Big deal. You had a really difficult year, and you gained twenty-seven pounds. So what? You're still you, the same person, and twenty-seven pounds is hardly the end of the world. *Just get back on track and get back to how you want to look and feel.* So you won't get there this week, or the next, or the next, but you can be there in several months. That's not that far away, and you can be feeling confident and beautiful and strong. So why not start practicing those feelings now—right now, at twenty-seven pounds more than you'd like to be weighing at the moment, especially since you're the same person inside no matter what the scale says. Just remember that you are confident and beautiful and strong right now. Your waistline will follow.

I wish I could say I wrote myself this letter and dropped eleven pounds by morning. Come to think of it, maybe I *can* say that. After all, when I gave myself the same measure of grace I'm willing to give my best friends, it sure lifted a load from my shoulders, even if it *didn't* alter my waistline.

Make Amends

"I'll never forgive myself for . . .

. . . not finishing college."
. . . telling him off like that."

. . . not explaining why I acted the way I did."
. . . breaking my promise to her."
. . . not setting things right when I had the chance."

Sometimes we can't go back and make amends. People move or die. Windows of opportunity close and lock tight. Time marches on, and the chance to amend a regret is gone, and only the task of forgiving ourselves remains.

But sometimes we *can* still make amends, and when we can, forgiving ourselves can turn from a burden to a joy.

Who says you can't finish your degree? Or apologize for something you said twenty years ago? Or correct an ancient misunderstanding, or keep a dusty promise, or set a wrong right?

Time marches on, it's true. But that doesn't mean it's never possible to run back and pick up something dropped along the way.

Respond As Wisely As Possible

Recently I read about a pastor who is stepping down from the ministry to seek professional and church counseling following a short-term homosexual relationship. He was quoted as saying, "As a minister of the gospel, I realize my moral failure has been inappropriate and wrong. I have asked God's forgiveness and for the past month have sought professional counseling and other help. I ask anyone affected by my actions to forgive me and to pray for both my spiritual and physical recovery."

A friend of mine commented, "Wow, his ministry will never be the same."

But I didn't come away with that thought. In fact, after reading the article, I wasn't thinking about his mistake at all. Instead, I appreciated the way the pastor responded to his failure with as much wisdom and integrity as he could muster. He brought his mistake into the light. He sought forgiveness from others, God, and hopefully from himself. He found psychologists and pastors to provide wisdom, strength, accountability, and prayers as he journeys back to wholeness and healing.

I don't know about you, but I'll be praying for this man and desiring God's blessing on his life and ministry.

No one gets through life unscarred by failure. How wisely we *respond*, however, can determine whether those failures impact us for a season, or define us for the rest of our lives.

Apologize to Yourself

When Annie couldn't even look at a picture of her younger self without cringing, she picked up the phone and made an appointment to see a Christian counselor. She told him that she just couldn't forgive herself for making the decision to marry when she did.

> No one gets through life unscarred by failure. How wisely we *respond*, however, can determine whether those failures impact us for a season, or define us for the rest of our lives.

Her counselor offered a strange suggestion. He told her to go home, look at a photo of herself at twenty-four, and have a conversation with the young woman represented in the picture. He said, "Tell her you understand that she was young and naïve, that she didn't know what the future would hold, that she did the best she could."

How interesting! You know the grace I was talking about? The kind of grace I recently extended to my chubby self? This guy asked Annie to show the same grace to her *younger* self.

And then he took it a step further. He added, "In this pretend conversation, imagine young Annie asking you to forgive her for the choice that she made all those years ago. Then see if you can find it in your heart to forgive her."

Annie went home and did as her counselor asked.

But a funny thing happened.

Annie says, "I started off mad. As I looked at that photo and began talking to the girl in the picture, I let her have it. I told her she had messed up my life in a royal fashion. I asked what she could possibly have been thinking! I ranted about how very unhappy I'd been for years.

"And then I admitted that I understood she hadn't been malicious. That she was simply young and naïve and that there was no way she could have known the pain that was in her future. And before long I was weeping. And then suddenly *I* was the one apologizing to *her*! I apologized for hating her, for abandoning her, for pushing her out of my life! And for the first time I realized how wrong I'd been to harbor such bitterness at myself for so many years. And then I imagined that she hugged me and told me it was alright, that she understood. And then the most amazing thing happened: *She* forgave *me*."

When you fight with a husband, relative, or friend, what brings reconciliation? Very often the keys that open the door to forgiveness and healing are these: a heart-to-heart conversation, a good dose of grace, and a sincere apology. Sometimes it doesn't even matter who apologizes. Sometimes the person who marched into the conversation determined to receive an apology ends up giving one instead. But my point is that these are very good keys. In fact, they're *so* good, they work just as well when the person you're mad at is *you*.

Follow in the Footsteps of the Master Forgiver

Spill the beans. Keep the broth. Be my own best friend. Make amends. Respond to my mistakes as wisely as possible. Apologize to myself. These help me when I'm having a difficult time loving myself in spite of my mistakes.

Something else that helps is this: I follow in the footsteps of the Master Forgiver.

As you already know, several years ago my marriage was in cardiac arrest. I could practically hear whatever guardian angel might have been assigned to our relationship shouting "Code Blue!" If heart paddles would have helped, I'm sure some would have materialized out of thin air.

That's when I hauled myself into Christian counseling. One day I walked into John's office with a long face and a heavy heart. Sitting across from him, I blurted, "I went into a chat room again this week and flirted with a total stranger."

He said, "Did you confess it? Ask God to forgive you?"

I squinted at him. "That's an interesting question. Actually, it never crossed my mind." Obviously my thoughts had been too preoccupied with beating myself up about it.

"Now's as good a time as any. Would you like to do it now?"

> "I went into a chat room again this week and flirted with a total stranger."

We bowed our heads. I said, "Okay, Lord, here I am, and I've managed to mess up again. I'm really sorry. I can't believe I even did that. I'm such a mess. Would you please forgive me? I know how much—"

"Whoa, hold up a minute," John said. "You're making this too hard. The Bible says in 1 John 1:9 that 'If we confess our sins, he is faithful and just and will forgive us our sins and purify us from all unrighteousness' (NIV). Confession is short. It's *I confess* and then fill in the blank. That's it. Simple. Wanna try again?"

"Lord, I confess that I flirted in a chat room. Would you please please *please* be willing to forg—"

"Karen, why are you begging? He's already told you he'll do it. You don't need to beg. Just thank him for what he's already done."

I wondered if somewhere an angel was holding a blackboard and shouting, "Take three!"

I tried again. I said, "Lord, I confess that I flirted in a chat room. Thank you for forgiving me. Amen." I looked up.

John said, "Feel better?"

"Yeah. But what if I mess up again?"

"Then you'll know what to say. Confess it and thank him for forgiving you."

And you know what? I really did feel better. What's more, it was a whole lot easier to forgive myself once I realized that Someone else had already blazed that trail before me.

And what an example he sets for me! If the King of Kings can forgive me without making me grovel, whine, bash myself, or beg, then what's *my* deal? Do I have more stringent standards than a holy God? Why do I demand something of myself that even *he* doesn't require?

I've met women who have said, "I've asked God to forgive me, and I believe that he has. But I just can't forgive myself."

I've thought a lot about that.

I've decided that it takes a lot of nerve to say that. To say, in essence, "I have higher standards than God."

I think something else happens when we can't forgive ourselves for something God has clearly forgiven, and it's this: We belittle what Jesus did for us on the cross.

> When it comes to my personal account in God's big book of goofs, across from every ugly deed I've ever committed—in the column that says "Amount Due"—there's scrawled in red a big fat zero.

What exactly did Jesus do? Here is the Cliff Notes version: Knowing that you and I would DEFINITELY mess up, Jesus turned to God, his Father, and said: "Let me take the punishment for those mistakes. I've got big shoulders. I can handle it. That way, when Karen and even _____ (fill in your name here) come to you down the line and say, 'Boy, did I ever mess up! I confess. Would you forgive me?' you can say *Yes*. Not *Well, sure, but there's this small matter of judgment and punishment to take care of,* but just a big welcoming *Yes!*"

The bad news is that I make mistakes. The good news is that Jesus paid a terrible and wonderful price so that I can be forgiven and with no strings attached! When it comes to my personal account in God's big book of goofs, across from every ugly deed I've ever committed—in the column that says "Amount Due"—there's scrawled in red a big fat zero.

If Christ's death on the cross is good enough for a Holy God, then it'd better be good enough for me!

So you can see I've been giving this a lot of thought. And one more thing came to mind. When you and I can't forgive ourselves for something that God has forgiven, we are stealing from God.

Once we confess our sins and receive his forgiveness, it makes sense that we would be filled with joy and relief and gratitude. And with all those incredibly good feelings bubbling around, it's natural for something else to bubble up and out of our happy hearts: Praise. Worship. Adoration. Thanksgiving. Gifts from our hearts to the heart of a merciful God.

But when you and I refuse to forgive ourselves, it throws a monkey wrench in the whole matter. God might have forgiven us, but we still can't let go of the emotional impact of our mistake, and as a result we're *not* joyful. Or relieved. Or thankful. And the only thing bubbling out of our hearts is self-condemnation. And maybe a little loathing.

But not praise. And certainly not worship or adoration or thanksgiving.

And the person we're withholding all that from happens to be God.

I don't know about you, but I'm thinking that maybe it's time to wave the white flag, show some grace, forgive myself, and move on with my life.

Besides, if my mistakes prove anything at all, it's that I'm alive and well on Planet Earth.

In fact, I'd wager that if a woman has no resume of mistakes, failures, and disappointments, she is (1) just pretending to be alive; (2) about as interesting as table salt; (3) the true queen of denial; (4) a close personal friend of Santa Claus and the Easter Bunny; and/or (5) extremely annoying to have as a friend.

Not to mention the fact that she'll never be able to break the ice at a party by announcing that she once got *both* her lips caught in a car door.

Karen Linamen is the author or coauthor of nine books and a contributing writer for *Today's Christian Woman* magazine. Formerly an editor with Focus on the Family and humor columnist for the Women of Faith web site, Karen is a frequent speaker at church and community women's events. She lives with her family in Littleton, Colorado.

To obtain information about having Karen speak at an event, contact Michelle Willett at ConnectionPointe Publicity Resources, mwillett@connectionpointe.com.

To get in touch with Karen (she always loves hearing from readers!), write to her at thefunnyfarm@email.com